Principles of Child Protection:
Management and Practice

Principles of Child Protection: Management and Practice

Anne Lawrence

Open University Press

Open University Press
McGraw-Hill Education
McGraw-Hill House
Shoppenhangers Road
Maidenhead, Berkshire
England SL6 2QL

email: enquiries@openup.co.uk
world wide web: www.openup.co.uk

and Two Penn Plaza, New York, NY 1012–2289
USA

First published 2004

A catalogue record of this book is available from the British Library

ISBN 0 335 21463 0 (pb)   0 335 21464 9 (hb)

Library of Congress Cataloging-in-Publication Data
CIP data has been applied for

Typeset by BookEns Ltd, Royston, Herts.
Printed and bound in Great Britain by
Bell & Bain Ltd, Glasgow

To
Patrick

Contents

Preface

Social work practice in child protection is on the brink of an exciting new future. Governmental reports, Acts of Parliament, the appointments of Commissioners and Ministers for Children have all provided a stimulus for a radical change in policy and organization. These events are discussed in this book, along with the challenges and major issues in practice and theory that have served as a catalyst for these developments. The principles of child protection services are analysed through a discussion of the main issues arising in both practice and theory.

The arguments surrounding the definitions of child abuse are outlined through an account of the phenomenon as an evolving social construction. The social factors that have led to the rise in the incidence of this phenomenon as well as the expansion of definitions of child abuse and child sexual abuse are critically examined. The nature of adult/child relationships is explored in terms of the varied social and cultural descriptions of childhood that have occurred over time. Specific attention is given to the rights of children and the professional regulation of child abuse and child sexual abuse in relation to the conceptual frameworks as defined by specific periods of history.

In order to understand the evolving pathway of child protection work, it is necessary to consider its origins in what had originally been referred to as 'child welfare practice'. The professional regulation of child abuse management operated within the medical model from the 1960s to the mid- to late 1980s. The pivotal Cleveland Report, following the child sexual abuse scandal in the north-east of England, was accompanied by a moral panic and a backlash in society against social workers and existing methods of professional regulation. History now records that the medical model that had dominated child abuse management was replaced by a socio-legal framework at this time. This change of emphasis heralded the emergence of a new discourse of child protection. Other notable child abuse tragedies occurred in England during the 1980s and regrettably have continued to the present day. As a direct result of these events, official inquiries were made, culminating in various government reports. Consequently, numerous and highly prescriptive government recommendations were made for the improvement of services.

Debates about the most effective methods of child protection management today are centred on the need for the adoption of a more culturally sensitive and subjectivist approach in the management of child abuse and children's welfare in general. Practice conflicts, interagency misunderstandings and other barriers to cooperation have always been major issues to be overcome in the child protection field. These surface problems are readily identifiable. However, there are underlying theoretical and sociological problems that are not so readily identified. Moreover, these problems are often the source of the expression of surface problems. Despite these impediments to practice there is evidence to support the view that the operation of interagency multidisciplinary responses to the management of children's welfare will continue albeit, in an altered form. The precise methods of organizing a new and effective service remain a huge challenge for all the participants in children's welfare.

It is hoped that this book will provide not only a source of reference for practitioners but will also provide an increased knowledge base for those working in this difficult and evolving profession. The book also aims to contribute to the status of the social work profession generally, not only through an increased knowledge base but also by attempting to secure practice with a sound theoretical foundation.

The impetus for this book arose from the experience of the author as a social work practitioner and manager working in the areas of children's welfare, child health and children's protection. This work was completed following work in the United States, England and Australia. The book draws upon and gives reference to personal examples of child welfare and child protection practice from these three countries.

Acknowledgements

I would like to acknowledge and thank all those who have contributed ideas and sentiments that helped to shape this book. I would like to acknowledge my social work colleagues and teachers over the years who have contributed their experiences with candour, pathos and often humour. I would specifically like to thank Professor David Thorpe for his insight and helpful references. This help proved to be a powerful impetus to the writing of this book.

A heartfelt thanks to my husband, Denis, for his keen insight, wisdom and suggestions while reviewing the final text of the book as well as for providing encouragement throughout its preparation. A special thank you to Len Baglow, who generously agreed to the use of his model for inter-agency cooperation to be reprinted in this book. I am indebted to Kieran O'Hagan for his scrutiny of the manuscript and his invaluable suggestions for amendments to the text. I also want to thank Rachel Gear at Open University Press for her enthusiastic support. A special note of gratitude goes to my daughter, Mary Anne, for providing crucial references on children's rights and legal issues and her expert guidance on computer technology that simplified the construction of the book. Thanks also to my son, Thomas, for his cheerful encouragement throughout.

A final acknowledgement and expression of gratitude must go to the children and families who have sought social work assistance and who have shared their difficulties and dreams for a better life.

Introduction

The problems of child abuse and its management have been of major concern in all western countries since the early 1960s and are now of truly international concern (Cooper and Ball 1987; Parton *et al*. 1997; Corby 2000). The need to ensure effective cooperation between different agencies involved in the management of child abuse has continually been highlighted in various official reports and government legislation such as the *Cleveland Report* (Butler-Sloss 1988), the UK Children Act 1989, *Working Together* (DoH 1991b), *Child Protection: Messages from Research* (DoH 1995) and more recently in the Green Paper *Every Child Matters* (DfES 2003). The importance of interagency multidisciplinary work was also acknowledged in these documents, as well as the serious consequences in the breakdown of interagency communications (Reder *et al*. 1993; Laming 2003).

Following the Cleveland Report, there began to be a change in emphasis away from a medical-scientific approach to the identification of child abuse and towards a more legalistic and evidential framework. This new approach continued with a pseudo-scientific approach, but the emphasis was now placed on the importance of joint work between the police and the social services in the investigations of child abuse. This legal framework, within which social work practitioners were to operate, brought with it a new construction and interpretation of investigation and the gathering of evidence. The 'child protection' discourse had now come into being, superseding 'child abuse' management. As the evidential processes of investigation became predominant, complexities and dilemmas about 'risk of abuse' and its management were introduced that confounded practitioners seeking to act in the best interests of the child (Dingwall *et al*. 1983; Wattam 1992; King 1997, 1999). Critics of this system believed that the traditional therapeutic role of the social worker was being called into question. The complexities and dilemmas for practitioners appeared to stem from the strictly positivistic approach that led to evidential information-gathering.

Although official recommendations and local reports upheld that coordination and cooperation between different agencies was necessary, they appeared not to recognize the complexities involved when such disparate groups of professionals are asked to work together (Hallett and Birchall 1992; Birchall and Hallett 1995). The planning, development and review of child protection services as a whole appeared not to be given its fullest consideration (Sanders *et al.* 1996). The underlying difficulties remained, and further issues became apparent in the regulation and management of child abuse. Wattam (1996) reviewed the landmark document *Child Protection: Messages From Research* (DoH 1995), from which she was able to distil a number of shortcomings that have come to be seen as major underlying issues needing clarification in this area of work. Problems relating to the definitions of child abuse, working in partnership with parents, and the continued preference of referring to 'children in need' as those at risk of abuse, rather than those identified with special needs, were among some of the issues highlighted by Wattam.

Research, as well as practice, was affected by the problems of definition, making it difficult to evaluate the results of various studies. This difficulty is most evident in terms of the lack of incidence and prevalence surveys. To this day the size of the problem remains relatively unknown because of the paucity of reliable statistics.

Despite these problems and the lack of attention given to the complexities underlying the tasks faced on a daily basis by practitioners, interagency organizational mechanisms were being put into place and policies were being developed. It is noteworthy that the attitudes and experiences of the professionals being asked to implement the policies were given scant recognition in their compilation (Parton 1985, 1991; O'Hagan 1989; Hallett and Birchall 1992; Hitchcock and Hughes 1992; Scott 1997).

Although the structures and procedures for interagency cooperation were being put into place in the early 1980s, it soon became clear that there were challenges and tensions in the management of child sexual abuse being experienced wherever this form of child abuse was being managed. The workers' tensions about their roles, the problems of intervening in the family life of others, the sharing of information with other agencies and difficulties surrounding acceptable amounts of risk because of no clear definitions of abuse, were all present. Practitioners were attempting to deal with risk assessments and frequently expressed concern among themselves and to their managers that their intervention might be considered inappropriate. This appeared to reflect their unwillingness to commit themselves to an action where there were no official guidelines.

In particular, there were many parallels regarding structures, systems and problems between England and Australia, in terms of the development of sexual abuse services for children (Bell 1988; Cambell 1988; Carmody 1990; Lawrence 1990). Among these were the reliance on the medical model, interagency conflict, professional rivalries and the increasing number of families who were seeking help. It was clear that although services in the management of child sexual abuse in both countries had many shared methods of operation, they also shared many of the same problems. Indeed, the same problems appeared to be present throughout the western world (Furniss 1983; Dale and Davies 1985; Lyon and Kouloumpos-Lenares 1987; Alaszewski and Harrison 1988; Anthony *et al.* 1988; Challis *et al.* 1988; Baglow 1990; Hallett and Birchall 1992; Cooper 1993; Buckley, *et al.* 1997). A lack of positive statements of operations in the management of child sexual abuse continues to be noted.

Although services were growing worldwide, it became apparent that there was little evaluative research into their effectiveness with regard to either clients or workers (Faller 1985; O'Hagan 1989; Stevenson 1989a; Scott 1997). The negative feedback from families and the media, high attrition rates among social workers and professional 'burnout', reinforced the need for research generally in this most difficult area of work (Armstrong 1979; Parton 1985; MacDonald 1990; Myers 1994). There were concerns about the rising number of cases being referred, as well as who should manage them and also how they should be managed. Additionally, there was concern about how all of the participants should behave for the greater good of all involved. These issues continue today to be at the centre of much debate (Myers 1994; King 1997, 1999; Parton *et al.* 1997; Houston and Griffiths 2000) and will no doubt continue until the results of reliable research are available.

Chapter 1 of this book presents a brief historical overview of the significant literature related to the evolving social construction of child abuse and child sexual abuse. The development of contemporary concerns about child sexual abuse and the issues associated with the rediscovery of this phenomenon are discussed. The heightened awareness in society of the problem of child sexual abuse in the late 1970s engendered a dramatic rise in the number and types of referrals bringing with it other, different problems, for the management of the phenomenon. Among these problems were those surrounding the ever-broadening definition of abuse, the influence of special interest groups on these definitions and the reification of the phenomenon. These new challenges facing child protection practitioners and managers are presented in Chapter 1, together with the issues concerning the interpretation of incidence and prevalence studies. The lack of consensus over definitions of child sexual abuse in the research literature and the effect that this has on the ability to obtain reliable research findings is also discussed. The epidemiological value of incidence and prevalence studies, along with statistical estimations in regard to the extent of child sexual abuse, conclude the chapter.

Chapter 2 provides an account of the evolving social construction of childhood. The traditional neglect of childhood as a sociological concept is

discussed. This is followed by an account of historical and cultural influences on the varying definitions of childhood. These historical divisions are
commonly referred to as the 'periodization' of childhood into respective
eras. This description begins with a discussion of the child in agricultural
society. Thereafter, it traces the development of the construction of childhood in the periods often referred to as 'modern' and 'late/advanced
modern', together with a discussion of the contemporary welfare child.
Notions of childhood innocence and the social anxiety these have created
are now part of the child protection discourse. These are discussed in relation to legislation and children's rights.

Chapter 3 presents a brief historical account of the growth and development of the child protection discourse, with particular reference to the shift
from a socio/medical paradigm to a legal one. The backlash against child
protection intervention that was a major factor in this change of emphasis
is discussed, together with the challenges it has presented to the contemporary system of child protection. Among these challenges are the dilemmas that have arisen in the identification and management of child sexual
abuse. These are discussed in the light of the need to avoid secondary
victimization of children and families. This is explored, together with the
impediments to establishing a professional relationship with children and
families that also recognizes their rights in relation to the responsibilities of
the state. The domination of the positivistic 'risk' assessment procedure
within the legal system of management has created pressure for an evidential focus in the investigation of child abuse and child sexual abuse,
often referred to as 'defensive practice'. The problems that this has created
for clients and practitioners are discussed in this chapter, which concludes
by raising the issue of whether the current child protection system tends to
review cases of abuse in terms of individual pathology and tends not to
address broader social factors such as chronic abuse caused by poverty.

Chapter 4 discusses the interagency, multidisciplinary approach associated with the professional regulation of child abuse, together with the problems and conflicts involved in this method of working. Two categories of
difficulty and possible conflict often generated in the interagency, multidisciplinary system are discussed. The first refers to the tensions and stresses
caused to those involved in the child protection process. This includes
practice conflicts, communication difficulties and barriers to interagency
cooperation. This first category is given the term 'surface conflicts'. The
second category refers to underlying theoretical challenges that need to be
acknowledged and accommodated. Within this category there is the
paradox created for the social work profession by having to make moralistic,
situated judgements, while at the same time being expected to work within
an objectivistic decision-making process. Also within the second category is
the need for practitioners to understand the role and function of closed

systems such as law, education and health. A knowledge of the inherent limits of these systems is necessary in order to achieve a balanced perspective for practice. Chapter 4 also contains a discussion of some of the key criticisms of the current child protection interagency method of working. These include a need to review the objectivist approach, gaps in services, eligibility criteria for services, imbalances in the system and the need for evaluation of services as well as further social research.

Chapter 5 emphasizes the need for social work practitioners and managers to have a sound theoretical basis for professional practice. A selection of major organizational perspectives on contemporary theories are discussed in relation to their influence on current social work and child protection practice. Some of the main postmodern influences on organizations involved in the child protection discourse are delineated. The chapter concludes by outlining the development of an integrated, eclectic approach contributing to a 'critical theory' of organizations, incorporating the various perspectives presented.

Chapter 6 makes recommendations for the future practice of children's welfare in the light of the major issues discussed in the preceding chapters. It advocates a broader welfare perspective for the inclusion of more children and families, including a more preventative role for practitioners in all of the children's services. It argues for a return to the more traditional values of the social work profession, with the emphasis on reflexive practice and the therapeutic relationship. Finally, it advocates the appointment of a Commissioner for Children and young people as well as a Minister for Children.

Chapter 7 provides an overview of the major issues discussed in this book. It recounts the value of the continuation of the interagency, multidisciplinary approach to the management of child abuse while identifying the difficulties within this system that need to be addressed. The need to broaden the focus of children's welfare services and to reappraise child protection practice is acknowledged. The chapter also emphasizes that society and government must be helped to recognize this need for change in order to avoid the mistakes of the past. A recognition of the need to rebalance services, as discussed in this book, would result in a rise in the status of social work as a profession and provide a unique role for the social work practitioner.

1 The evolving social construction of child abuse and child sexual abuse

Introduction

The maltreatment of children by adults has existed from time immemorial, and is recorded in the history of ancient societies all over the world. While the cruel treatment of children has been well documented in history, the literature also refers to the 'newness' of the problem of child abuse (Archard 1999). This apparent contradiction reflects the medical-scientific identification of child physical trauma that began in America in the 1950s.

A decade after this early research into physical injuries, the 'Battered Child Syndrome' was used in western societies to describe the phenomenon of child abuse. This 'rediscovery' of child abuse was credited to the eminent paediatrician Dr Henry Kempe and his associates at the University of Colorado in Denver. It was after the publication and dissemination of their results that 'child abuse' began to be acknowledged as a social problem (Kempe *et al.* 1962; Gordon 1985; Parton 1985; Parton *et al.* 1997). An ever-broadening recognition of the types of abuse and a concern for the problems to be managed has been emerging ever since.

Over time, there have been many different definitions of the phenomenon, and child abuse is now perceived as an evolving social construction. The reification and ever-broadening dimensions of child abuse are presented in this chapter. The need to define child abuse is discussed in reference to the contemporary employment of orthodox positivistic definitions and their reliance on risk assessment procedures.

Myths, legends and incest taboos have been recorded over time as a testimony of the deep-seated societal recognition of child-adult sexual relationships and a need for their regulation. Nevertheless, even though

child sexual abuse has had this long history and had also been acknowledged as unlawful for many decades, it was not until the 1960s that the
issue began to gain widespread social attention (Howitt 1992). The significant events in the development of the concept of child sexual abuse and
the societal issues associated with its 'rediscovery' will be discussed. During
the 1970s and into the 1980s there were many attendant problems arising
from the phenomenon, such as the need to cope with the increasing
number of referrals, and the media glare on what were deemed to be professional failures to protect children.

The definitions of child sexual abuse together with the influence of
special interest groups upon the construction of definitions are reviewed.
These special interest groups often had contradictory theories relating to
the causes of child sexual abuse, with each providing their own definition
of the problem. Many of these competing definitions have produced problems that have created different emphases in the intervention, treatment
and prevention of abuse, and are considered to be at the core of child sexual
abuse management (Howitt 1992; Parton *et al.* 1997). The lack of consensus
on definitions has also been problematic when comparing research findings
based on incidence, prevalence and epidemiological studies, and this will
also be reviewed.

Definitions of child abuse

Despite all the attention and interest shown in the topic, it is curious that
at the present time there is no substantive definition for child abuse. There
are many definitions, and they are fraught with both cultural and value-
based difficulties. Parton *et al.* (1997) reported that during the previous
two decades there had been little progress made in constructing a clear,
concise, reliable, valid and agreed-upon definition of child abuse. It would
seem that the problem of arriving at a definition was exacerbated by an
ever-changing conceptual basis of abuse.

Child abuse is so familiar a term that it is difficult to understand and
accept that there is no substantive definition for it. Children are known to
suffer deliberate harm at the hands of caregivers and others. It is known
that child abuse exists. This familiarity with the concept is part of its con-
tentiousness, as everyone feels that they know what constitutes child abuse,
although there is no consensus on definition. However, how it is defined,
and how professional child protection workers react to it, are directly
related to the definitions applied. The ongoing debate in contemporary
society about the role of corporal punishment in childrearing practices is
one example of the difficulty faced when trying to define child abuse. There
are those who would consider that children who are smacked are suffering
child abuse and those who consider it to be a normal aspect of childrearing.

The term 'child physical abuse' conceals a culturally embedded and assumed belief system about childrearing practices (Thorpe and Jackson 1997). It may be that legislation is necessary to clarify the situation. It is quite remarkable that in the year 2004 the United Nations has only recently expressed concern that the UK has not taken significant action in prohibiting the corporal punishment of children in the family.

In the light of such criticism it would seem to be only a matter of time before corporal punishment will be made illegal. It would certainly be in the interests of children to make smacking and all forms of corporal punishment illegal acts. Apart from presenting to the child an 'undesirable model', there is always the potential for serious injury as well as the possibility of lowered self-esteem.

Legislation making smacking an illegal act would also help to clarify the definition of child physical abuse. However, as pointed out by Thorpe and Jackson (1997), smacking a child is bound up with cultural and value-laden issues that contribute to the ongoing debate concerning this emotionally riven topic. The debate over whether to legislate against domestic corporal punishment is a sensitive one in that it is central to the quality of the parent-child relationship and concerns the right of the state to intervene in family life. Within this context, the achievement of a consensus over the definition of child abuse is fraught with problems.

Once it is accepted that child abuse is an interactional process and has to be viewed in the context of a social interaction it follows that there will be various dimensions of possible child abuse within the parent-child relationship (Zeedyk 1998). The cases of obvious parental assault on vulnerable children within the family are easily understood.

Not so easily understood is the phenomenon of children actually inciting child abuse from their parents. Boss (1980) points out that some children who may be born with various special needs place undue strain on the parent-child relationship and parents may become frustrated and disappointed with their child. Boss describes, as an example, an underweight baby who does not thrive, is irritable and cries excessively. Another example is where the baby may be separated from the mother in the early postpartum period. This latter example is said to have the effect of lowering the mother's self-confidence when eventually reunited with her child. In such situations the child's needs would tend to be neglected. Many parents in such a situation will bring their child to a hospital for help, expressing concern over the child's difficult behaviour and their fears that they may harm the child. Parents attending parenting workshops also express these same fears about their children's behaviour and their own negative reactions to it. This notion of a child indirectly inciting abuse is referred to by Boss (1980: 57) as 'the child as a defenceless victim'.

Archard (1999: 82) has commented on the fact that the 'newness' of the term of 'child abuse' has meant that it is a 'human kind' term. That is, it is one that has been constructed rather than being steeped in a 'natural kind' of history with the advantage of long-standing usage. The term is thus malleable and easily reconstructed. Archard also comments that this newness allows its definitions to be commandeered by a variety of interest groups, each with its own definition that will imply a causal explanation. If a group can claim to understand the etiology of the phenomenon then perhaps this group alone can claim to have the resources to understand it and act.

In relation to defining child abuse, Gough (1996: 993) has said that 'An examination of the meaning of the concept may be seen, at best, as an important but rather tedious and technical issue and, at worst, as an over-intellectual questioning of the meaning of abuse that implies that abuse does not really exist.' Gough goes further to say that despite all the work that has been done in the area of definitions, there has been no framework to integrate it into a coherent body of knowledge.

Wattam (1996) also recognizes this deficit by referring to the lack of expansion and discussion of definitional issues in *Child Protection: Messages from Research* (DoH 1995). While agreeing with this document that child abuse is not an absolute concept, Wattam criticizes the report on the grounds that it attempts to reconstruct a consensual definition of abuse based on moral concerns along a continuum of behaviours, seemingly ignoring other perspectives such as the legal or the scientific. The lack of specificity in the definition of abuse has resulted in generalizations, often based on moralistic grounds alone. The dangers of this approach are only now being acknowledged as possibly harmful in themselves.

The relative nature of the conceptualization of child abuse means that it is a culturally specific, legal and moral judgement. To view the phenomenon of child abuse as socially constructed does not mean that the definitions are relative *per se*. It does, however, imply that a definition must be achieved on each and every occasion of practical application, to judge if abuse has occurred (Parton *et al.* 1997). This contentious area may be demonstrated by the following example from experience of the author.

> In the mid-1960s, while working as a new graduate in the city of Chicago, I was employed as a caseworker for the Cook County Public Aid Department. The caseworker's role was to make quarterly visits to clients in receipt of welfare benefits, called at that time 'Aid to Dependent Children'. The task then was to review the general health and welfare of recipients and to inquire if the monthly benefit was adequate for the monthly expenditure. Each worker had an assigned 'district' and mine was an older city neighbourhood of impoverished, derelict, subdivided apartments.

On one freezing day's visit to the 'district' I came across a 5-year-old boy in a shop doorway. He was inadequately dressed, begging for handouts and appeared to be suffering from cold or flu. In an effort to assist I made enquiries in the store to see if they knew him or his background. I was told that his parents were at work. The parents were said to have locked him out of the house when they went to work as they thought that was safer than his being in the home on his own. In discussion with my supervisor I was told that there was nothing I could do as I had no jurisdiction over those not in receipt of welfare payments. The subject was closed. Later that week I received a telephone call from an irate policeman who said that he had witnessed an extremely neglected child in my district and asked what was I doing about it. I explained that as the parents were in private employment I could not intervene, but that I was glad to know that the police were taking the matter seriously. The policeman changed his demeanour immediately and said that he was relieved to know that the parents of the child in question were not squandering taxpayers' money. The child and his family were not 'welfare cases'. As long as it was a private family matter he would accept that he had no right to intervene.

In the mid-1960s there was less sensitivity to cases of 5- and 6-year-olds in need of care and attention than there is today. If the child's parents in my example had been on welfare, things might have been different. The neglected child might have wondered why the professionals involved looked so helplessly at him. In later days in the district the boy would often be in the houses of nearby neighbours where he ate and played with others of his age. One of the women in whose house he appeared explained that they all knew the boy, he was a 'stray' and that, in the end, somebody would look after him. There was the objective reality of a suffering child, but the situation did not come under any official category of abuse and so no official action could be taken. This example illustrates how definitions of abuse and neglect have changed since the 1960s.

Reification of the term 'child abuse'

The term 'child abuse' is widely used, and the lack of specificity in its definition generally ignored. This lack of clarity has contributed to the use of emotive images of children by various charities for fundraising appeals (Archard 1999). The result has been to turn child abuse into a marketable commodity. In addition, this type of conception of abuse has contributed to a process of reification of the term, with sensationalized dramatizations of the victim's condition evoking horror, guilt and shame. So powerful are these emotional appeals that, as Gough (1996: 994) commented, 'Even some adults who involve children in sexual relations are against child abuse'.

Today, the reification of the term 'child abuse' as a universal identifiable phenomenon is widespread (Adler 1996; Gough 1996). However, the definition of the term is gradually changing in the literature and it is now perceived as one of cultural relativism (Parton *et al.* 1997). As such, the phrases that refer to child abuse and child sexual abuse are now being discussed in the literature as 'social constructions' (Wattam 1992, 1996; Reder *et al.* 1993; Parton *et al.* 1997; Archard 1999; King 1999). Although legislation has made explicit the unlawfulness of certain behaviours and omissions of behaviour as crimes against children, the identification and prevention of abuse is not always straightforward, and is often fraught with subjective judgements and moralistic risk assessments (Parton *et al.* 1997).

It is not surprising to discover, therefore, that there are eminent authorities on this topic who would recommend alternative terms to the word 'abuse'. For example, words such as 'harm', 'injury' and 'maltreatment' (Wattam 1992, 1996; Gough 1996; Parton *et al.* 1997; King 1997, 1999; Archard 1999). However, although there remains no general consensual definition, this is not to say that the term 'abuse' is not sometimes useful as an appropriate description of maltreatment. After all, the term is in the common vocabulary and in the literature on children and their welfare. Archard (1999) has also pointed out that it would be a conceit to think that a simple clarification of a definition would remedy what has come to symbolize a vast array of problems and misconceptions.

It may be that a more open and sympathetic approach to the description of a range of difficulties is required in order to understand the dimensions of child abuse facing practitioners. In the meantime, the difficulties of definition remain and the use of the term continues to be debated.

The broadening of the dimensions of child abuse

The dimensions of child abuse have broadened since the 1960s, and contemporary literature on child abuse now refers to the phenomenon as an evolving social construction, as mentioned above (Reder *et al.* 1993; Wattam 1996; King 1999). Gough (1996) outlined six areas where this growth has evolved. First, there has been an expansion in the types of abuse in line with the stages of societal awareness in the pattern described by Henry Kempe (1979) – from the 'Battered Baby Syndrome', to physical abuse of children, failure to thrive, neglect, emotional abuse and sexual abuse. Second, there has been a recognition of the broadening range of people who might be held responsible for abuse. The scope has increased from primary caregivers through to strangers, institutional and educational abuse and the secondary victimization of children by 'system-induced trauma' (Conte 1984). Chapter 3 contains a section devoted to this particular topic, wherein the child protection investigation and subsequent intervention may create more problems than it has solved. Third, the expansion of consideration as to what may be appropriate care for the satisfactory development of children's mental health has expanded to consider the effects of such things as parental discord, domestic violence and divorce. Fourth, there has been a growth in concerns for children's rights and their inability to give informed consent in matters such as sexual activity with adults and access arrangements in cases of parental separation. Fifth, there has been the construction of the duration of childhood as being from conception to the (often arbitrary) cut-off age where adulthood is supposed to begin. Lastly, the combination of increased prosperity, together with the above factors, has contributed to a general lowering of criteria as to what is considered to be abusive. As people in the developed world attain higher standards of living, expectations of care increase and so a 'higher order' of abuse can come into being (Cooper 1993: 2). For example, it was not uncommon, in days gone by, for children to be seen working in factories, whereas today in the western world it would be considered to be abusive.

With regard to the higher order of care standards, it could be argued that some institutions in society have indirectly retarded progress towards children's general welfare by not readily accepting responsibility for children's health and well-being, or the apparent lack of it. One example of this is the apparently self-seeking pursuit of particular institutions, such as some international business conglomerates, who continue to market products aimed at children, knowing that they could be harmful to health. For example, food products containing excessive levels of salt, fat and sugar.

A further example is where some governmental policies appear to be economically motivated and give low priority to welfare programmes. The British Psychological Society's paper on child protection (2003) points out that 'children are vulnerable to abuse whenever their disabilities go unsupported'. The debates about the welfare and rights of children bring in moral issues which some say cannot be attributed to such governmental programmes (Archard 1999). There are also those who debate whether we can expect any of society's institutions to operate other than within their own closely defined parameters (King 1997). These arguments challenge the assumption that we can assert with any confidence what is universally in the best interests of children.

The broadening of the types of abuse, the age range of potential victims, and the increase of alleged perpetrators, have all contributed to the problem of defining child abuse. Hallett and Birchall (1992: 113) summarize the difficulties involved by saying that there are problems with the characterization of different types of insult as abuse, with different 'thresholds of seriousness' and with different actors as abusers, as well as difficulties in diagnosing specific incidents.

The task of making decisions in such situations is the central problem facing child protection practitioners.

Why the need to define child abuse?

The main reason for attempting to define 'child abuse' is to enhance the welfare of children by detecting and eliminating abuse (Archard 1999). The terms in which we talk about the problem are said to be crucially important for the ways in which we might think of solving it. The definitional issues and the problems that they can create are at the heart of child protection work. As discussed above, one of the probable reasons why there is no real consensus on definitions is the variety of forms that child abuse can take. Any behaviour may be considered to be 'abusive' if practitioners define it as such.

While many books show that there are a variety of definitions of child abuse, it is significant that they all characteristically arrive at a definition for their particular purpose (Parton *et al.* 1997). Whether the purpose is for practice, research or advocacy, each has a different definition. However, these definitions usually do share some common pattern (Archard 1999). Archard suggests that the definition most often quoted in government reports and official documents will tend to become the 'umbrella definition', also known as the 'orthodox narrow definition'. The phenomenon is said to have four sub-categories, each with its own definition, under the overall umbrella of 'child abuse'. These four categories are: physical abuse, physical neglect, sexual abuse and emotional abuse. Although neglect and emotional abuse are cited as separate categories, it could be argued that they are common to all types of abuse. Further amplification of these definitions can be found in *Working Together to Safeguard Children* (DoH 1999). The orthodoxy of these definitions stems from the fact that in theory, they represent episodes of serious forms of maltreatment. However, definitions of abuse can remain problematic for practitioners. The real-life episodes that are the day-to-day work of practitioners are not always so clearly defined, particularly as there are degrees of harm within these categories. Moreover, child abuse does not necessarily have overt signs.

In the mid-1980s, the need for precision in definition became less of a priority as the emphasis shifted from 'child abuse work' to 'child protection work', and the notion of 'risk assessment' was introduced. There was now a need for the development of new sets of procedures, policies and legislation that would introduce a broader remit for practitioners. In Britain, this was the result of a series of inquiries concerning publicly highlighted child abuse deaths, and the *Cleveland Report* (Butler-Sloss 1988). There had been a moral outpouring of anger at social workers for failing to do their work in preventing child abuse tragedies, and this was seen to be in need of rectification through new legislation.

What had been considered to be the objectifiable, medical-scientific phenomenon of 'child abuse' as presented in the 1960s had altered over the years to become more legalistic and socially preconceived, often formulated in terms of risk assessment. This has come to represent a fundamental shift in the pattern of the societal regulation for the child protection discourse, to accommodate a more legalistic and morally judgemental set of social constructions (Wattam 1992; Buckley *et al*. 1997; King 1997). In this climate it is difficult to obtain a consensus on definitions, creating difficulties not only for practice, but also when researching the phenomenon of child abuse.

The appearance of the categorization of risk assessments followed the positivist paradigm that was first established in respect of defining abuse. That is, medical research established the nature of child abuse and the medico-scientific reality of child abuse was accepted. Medical science was seen as crucial for establishing the reliable formulation of generalizable knowledge about child abuse (Parton 1985). However, child abuse is difficult to define and the physical substantiation of some forms of abuse is acknowledged to be often impossible to obtain.

As mentioned above, the constructions of 'risk' of abuse and its 'measurement' have entered the child protection discourse in an attempt to balance 'unsubstantiated' yet suspected instances of possible harm to children. That is, where an allegation is not matched by forensic evidence or evidential criteria there is an alternative practice which involved assembling a list of certain contestable signs which may or may not predict that abuse might have happened or may be likely to happen. Achieving a balance with these factors is rarely a reliable or valid scientific activity, despite the desire for it to be so.

A further problem is that there seems to be a desire to defend the constructions of the positivistic paradigm in order to be confident that the 'right' action has been taken. This is sometimes referred to in the physical sciences as 'paradigm blindness', as the investigator does not see outside a prescribed framework. The decisions that follow are often open to much criticism on the grounds of being false and, often in the child protection system, as failing to protect children. The paradox of the difficulty of making what appear to be defensible, positivist decisions has become identified as being at the heart of the social work role in child protection matters. There is a case for greater acknowledgement of the social construction of the definitions of child abuse and child sexual abuse. A discussion of these socially constructed terms now follows.

The evolving social construction of child sexual abuse

There have been changes over time in the societal regulation of child-adult sexual relationships, the acknowledgement of child sexual abuse and the condemnation of the problem. These changes can be seen as part of wider changes in the spheres of economics and politics, such as the development of information technology and the changes in legislation allowing the state to intervene in child protection issues. The sociocultural responses these changes have created have continued with simultaneous ever-changing formulations. Leonard (1997) invites us to see that all of these forces are mutually determining and that one force cannot be analysed in isolation from the others. This can be appreciated from a brief historical overview of the development of child-adult sexual regulation.

This overview is intended to clarify the relativism of the social construction of child sexual abuse in the following ways. First, a historical overview makes clear how the facts and assumptions concerning the problem have been constructed and consequently the way they have structured policy and practice (Parton 1985). Second, if we can account for the causes of an issue identified as demanding action, in principle it is possible to do something about the problem (Parton 1985). Finally, reviewing the history of the topic may help to create a better understanding of the range of perspectives on the problem and increase sensitivity to the variety of societal and professional reactions a child protection practitioner might encounter.

Throughout history, there has been recorded in every society some degree of regular human maltreatment of other people, whether we are speaking of children or adults. However, societal acceptance of this maltreatment has varied over time, especially with regard to child sexual abuse. The sexual role ascribed to children has also varied over time. Therefore, it is not surprising to discover that the phenomenon of child sexual abuse has had a long and diverse history (De Mause 1974; Wattam 1992; Gough 1996; Jenks 1996; Achard 1999).

The sexual regulation of children has been part of social life since antiquity (De Mause 1974). The universality of an incest taboo is one example of such societal regulation. Some anthropologists have considered that incest taboos were established for the preservation of totems or clans; that is, to guarantee the survival of a specifically designated lineage and the distribution of property. Often taboos did not prohibit sexual relations between close blood ties on an equal biological basis. That is, one might be prohibited from forming a liaison with a paternal cousin but encouraged to form such a bond with the equivalent maternal blood tie relation. Many such specifications were made for the survival of a particular lineage and the strict distribution of inherited property. Some would argue that totems were ascribed to specific groupings of people for the preservation of the species itself, in so far as ascribing totems was originally conceived to deter cannibalism and was eventually extended to include sexual sanctions and prohibitions (Graburn 1971; Knight 1991; Featherstone *et al.* 1993).

History provides us with many accounts of what, today, we would call child sexual abuse (Ariès 1962; Gelles 1987; Jenks 1996). In ancient Greece, young boys experienced sexual activity with older men that was considered a form of educational instruction (Grimal 1965). Grimal also highlights the case of Victorian child flower-sellers, many of whom were said to be working as prostitutes. Child sexual abuse in these instances was culturally accepted and even sanctioned. As late as 1900, there were people who believed venereal disease could be cured by means of sexual intercourse with children (De Mause 1974: 49). In some parts of the world child prostitution continues as a business, although it is no longer overtly condoned by society (Vittachi 1989; Lansdown 1995; Newell 1995; Jenks 1996).

The first report of sexual abuse as a major hazard to child health is said to have occurred in the nineteenth century in France (DHSS 1988). It would seem this was the first modern acknowledgement of child sexual abuse as being of professional concern. The work was credited to Ambrose Tardieu, Professor of Legal Medicine in Paris, whose published findings in 1857 described thousands of cases of child sexual abuse (Myers 1994: 21). Myers quotes Summit (1988) to the effect that Tardieu's belief in sexual abuse was rejected by his successors.

The second major professional acknowledgement of child sexual abuse occurred in 1896, when Freud presented his seduction theory to the Vienna psychiatric establishment (Howitt 1992). It is said that Freud's peers similarly rejected his ideas. Freud abandoned his seduction theory and thereafter claimed that children were traumatized not by actual sexual abuse, but by projections of their own fantasies (Finklehor 1982).

Both of these professional entries are often viewed as case studies of theories of child sexual abuse that came into prominence only to be quickly submerged and ultimately rejected by ideological scepticism. These two examples also show that there was a reluctance to accept the word of the patients, who happened to be women or children. Further to this, in the history of professional involvement in child sexual abuse, there appears to have been a series of acceptances and denials of the problem.

Prior to the latter half of the twentieth century, the most striking feature of the history of child abuse and child sexual abuse has been the intermittent nature of public concern (Parton 1985). As far as child sexual abuse is concerned, perhaps this pattern is due to what Myers (1994: 23) refers to as society's 'blind spot for child sexual abuse' wherein the current 'discovery' of the problem is nothing more than the latest in a series of rediscoveries. Jenks (1996) commented on this same phenomenon, contending that the erotic element in child-adult relationships that today has been newly articulated is in fact nothing new. He added that, 'as Freud discovered, it has never been a dimension of human experience that dares to speak its name too loudly' (p. 88).

In the past, the taboos against incest and child sexual abuse led welfare workers and social researchers to be wary of asking questions about this activity to parents or children (Giddens 1993). Giddens also commented that many instances of the problem came to light once the topic was introduced into the public arena by the women's movement and child protection discourse. Thus, not only is the evolving phenomenon of child abuse itself open to definitional debate, but also the nature of the child-adult relationship is generally accepted to rest on the prevalent societal construction of childhood at any one time. The twin considerations of definitions of abuse and the social construction of childhood have extensive implications for the identification and management of the problem in both practice and theory. The varying constructions often dictate the standard of acceptable relations with children.

As child sexual abuse is an evolving social construction, it can be seen that behaviour sanctioned and tolerated in one time and place can evolve to be condemned and reviled in another. There have been many recorded examples in history of the sexual maltreatment of children that today would be called 'child sexual abuse'. However, it is only during the last 30 years that there has been an overwhelming societal condemnation of the problem (Finkelehor 1982; Cooper and Ball 1985; Parton 1985, 1991; Howitt 1992; Cooper 1993; Jenks 1996).

There can exist, even within one culture, a range of situations where the term 'child sexual abuse' is highly contentious and the protection of children difficult. The relativism of the term 'child sexual abuse' has not diminished in the modern world, even though the act is condemned. While acknowledging that harmful events happen to children, we need to be clear about why and how we define these events as abuse and look to the effect that our professional intervention may induce. There is little doubt from recorded history that what today would be called 'child sexual abuse' has always existed.

The development of contemporary concerns about child abuse and child sexual abuse

In describing the development of contemporary concerns about child abuse, Adler (1996) divided the past century into three broad epochs. He commented that around the turn of the twentieth century, formal laws for the protection of children appeared for the first time in the western world. The nineteenth-century moral campaigns for children were made acceptable to politicians when new concepts about children and the state's right to intervene in family life emerged (Piper 1999). A second epoch, comprising 50 to 60 years, followed wherein laws were used to protect children from 'neglectful' families, while the problems of child physical and sexual abuse were largely undisclosed (Adler 1996). This period saw the proliferation of institutionalized residential care for children who were orphaned, abandoned or neglected, organized by both state and voluntary concerns, in both England and Australia. Physical abuse and sexual abuse were not prominent issues at this time.

Adler (1996) points to the publication of the landmark works of John Bowlby (1951, 1969) in the UK, and Henry Kempe in the USA, as pivotal to the thinking at the time. Bowlby emphasized the importance of children having a consistent and loving relationship with a primary caregiver in the interests of their future mental health, and his work was said to have led to a widespread move away from institutional care.

The third epoch, following the influence of Bowlby and Kempe, brings the history of child care to its present child protection phase. This period was characterized by the identification of abuse and the assessment of possible risks of harm to children. Children were again being removed from their homes, but this time to substitute care arrangements, mostly in foster homes for varying periods of time. The dilemma that our current system is now said to face is that protecting children from actual harm can bring other, sometimes negative consequences brought about by a child's removal from their family home. This dilemma, among several other issues such as instances of further abuse while in foster care, has caused current practices to be questioned in the child protection discourse. There has been a gradual awareness of the uncertainties and ambiguities inherent in acting in the 'best interests' of children as conceived in the positivist paradigm of contemporary practice.

The rediscovery of child sexual abuse

The brief historical overview has demonstrated that while the subject of child-adult sexual relations is not new, the terms 'child abuse' and 'child sexual abuse' are the product of the debate begun by Kempe and his associates in the 1960s (Parton 1985; Adler 1996; Gough 1996; Jenks 1996; Parton *et al.* 1997). While the phenomenon of child maltreatment has always existed, Kempe's work brought child abuse to the forefront of the orthodox child protection discourse. As predicted by Kempe (1979), the more severe forms of physical abuse have been seen to precede the recognition of child sexual abuse and emotional abuse (Reder *et al.* 1993; Gough 1996; Parton *et al.* 1997). So it was that interest in the phenomenon of child sexual abuse did not become a matter of widespread social concern in the western world until the later half of the twentieth century (Cooper 1993).

Kempe and Kempe (1978) noted that the history of the emergence of any form of child abuse as a social issue involves three factors: first, a growing recognition of maltreatment as an unnecessary evil; second, the technical capability to identify clues that tell the story of inflicted injury; and third, the community's readiness to address the problem constructively.

Parton's (1985) approach develops this theme further when he says that we need to consider how far the concepts of moral enterprise, bureaucratic imperatives and symbolic action help to explain why child abuse was recognized as a problem at a particular time. He also adds that it is doubtful that these factors are sufficient as explanatory variables. Parton expresses the feeling that one must locate the reaction to child abuse within a theory of power; that is, within shifts in the economy and in ideological forces in society.

With these two perspectives in mind, it is interesting to note that Howitt (1992) complements both as he presents a historical account of child abuse and child sexual abuse by tracing the development of professionalism. More specifically, he traces how and when professionals began their role as authorities in childrearing practices in the nineteenth century. Howitt makes specific reference to the rising technical capabilities that were, at that time, in the hands of the professionals, particularly in the fields of religion, medicine and law. The same has applied to the evolving role of social work, accentuated by the media's reporting and the expansion of contemporary child protection systems as they interact with changes in legislation.

Commercial and professional interests are seen today to combine to keep the topic of childhood and child sexual abuse in the forefront of public interest. The National Society for the Prevention of Cruelty to Children (NSPCC), incest survivors' groups, Child Line, children's rights campaigns, and parental rights groups are but a few of the interested parties that keep the broad issues of child abuse to the fore in society. Additionally, international conferences on child abuse and neglect are now attended by representatives from many countries all over the world. These conferences regularly take place in both the northern and the southern hemispheres and to date, 12 biennial international congresses have been sponsored by the International Society for Prevention of Child Abuse and Neglect (ISPCAN). New professional journals on various aspects of the phenomenon are also on the increase and are adding to the professional debates concerning child abuse.

There have been a variety of changes in cultural attitudes and values over the decades that have brought about increased public interest in child sexual abuse. The recognition of child sexual abuse as a social problem that began in the late 1960s is said to have come about mainly as a result of the coalition of the women's movement and the child protection movement

(Finklehor 1982; Campbell 1988; Carmody 1990). There were many other societal changes occurring at the same time as the rise in recognition of child sexual abuse as a contemporary social problem that were also thought to be partly responsible. Some of these included those societal changes following World War II occurring in the community, the family, the status of marriage and the re-evaluation of established sex roles (Finklehor 1982). However, why concerns about childhood and child sexual abuse became a major political/social phenomenon goes beyond what were first perceived as simple explanations of evolving social institutions (Jenks 1996).

The increase in advocates of children's rights, the growth of the child protection industry, child abuse inquiries and the backlash of parents' groups against the child protection system were also contributing factors to highlighting the problem. All of the above changes in society and the rise in specialist interest groups 'reflect and feed into an emerging configuration of governmentality associated with "advanced liberal" societies' (Parton 1998: 6). All of these political, legal, economic and social factors combined to provide the backdrop for the rise of concern about child sexual abuse as a social problem, and continue to influence the evolving discourse of child abuse.

Problems stemming from societal recognition of child sexual abuse

Following the recognition of child sexual abuse as an issue of social concern in the late 1960s, it assumed political notoriety throughout the western world. This resulted in changes to legislation in both the United Kingdom and Australia and a problem to be managed by childrens' services (Boss 1980; Parton 1985, 1998; Howitt 1992; Myers 1994; Thorpe 1994). In these ensuing years, Skaff (1988) noted that the goals of child abuse and neglect services broadened from a relatively simple process of report, investigation, protection of children, and punishment of perpetrators, to include broader dimensions of prevention and rehabilitation for victims *and* perpetrators.

Among the problems that were generated by the increased societal interest in child sexual abuse were the growing numbers of cases reported and that needed to be managed. It is well documented that referrals of child sexual abuse grew exponentially from the 1960s (Sgroi 1982; Cooper and Ball 1987; Hallett and Birchall 1992; Howitt 1992). Contributing to the rise in the number of proven cases reported were those cases of 'possible' abuse where there was only a suspicion of abuse. Also contributing to this rise in incidence were cases of false reporting, some of which were subsequently revealed either to have been instances of Munchausen's Syndrome By Proxy (fictitious illness by proxy) (Horwath 1999), or of intended malicious origin.

There were also several other sources contributing to the increase in referrals. Increased numbers were reported in respect of a rise in the number of parental disputes over access rights after divorce. It is not uncommon for parents to make allegations of sexual abuse against each other and their respective new partners. Additionally, there are many instances of child sexual abuse occurring in daycare centres, schools and religious institutions. Following such referrals many children and their parents need to be interviewed.

Allegations of 'ritual' or 'satanic' abuse also increased in number and presented further problems for management (Wattam 1992; Corby 2000). This form and many other forms of alleged sexual abuse have remained a contentious area for management by professionals, as the accuracy of such claims has often been difficult to substantiate. Rarely have the presenting criteria concerning these allegations been sufficient for legal presentation, but at the same time such allegations have required investigation.

Psychotherapy saw an increase in cases of alleged sexual abuse with the emergence of 'Recovered Memory Syndrome' – that is, the delayed recall of child sexual abuse in adulthood. Critics considered this recall often to be false and there followed profound debate and controversy among the public and mental health professionals (Conway 1997; Courtois 1997). The counter stance suggested that clinicians might have been implanting misinformation or illusory memories in certain vulnerable clients (Yapko 1997).

The lack of clarity about child sexual abuse and the ability to manage the related issues it has generated have been telling indicators that most research in this area has been at a rudimentary level (Parton *et al.* 1997). Practitioners have been informed by epidemiological studies that no section of society can be exempted from the risk of possible sexual maltreatment of children. The risk of sexual abuse became a reality to be managed.

As the problem of child sexual abuse came into focus, attendant and less clear issues also arose. As an example, in the UK, the media, pressure groups, political representatives and Parliament all recognized that child protection issues were not neutral activities, but were riven by different values about the role of the family, the nature of state intervention, and the rights of children and their parents (Parton 1985). The Children Act 1989 was created as a legislative attempt to reach a balance between such diverse values and perspectives. The Act was recognized in the UK as *the* major childcare legislative event of the 1980s (Fox Harding 1991a: 179).

Among the achievements credited to the Act was the fact that it was seen to draw together clear links between public concerns, social policy and legislation. These links had been achieved in a non-partisan manner, which represented a high degree of consensus between political and professional bodies (Fox Harding 1991a). On the international stage, the United Nations *Declaration of the Rights of the Child* (1989) was a further example of a new approach to the issue of children's rights. The *Declaration* was regarded by some as a unique document on the treatment of children, their protection and their participation in society (Franklyn 1995b). International ratification of this document has been largely supported by United Nations' members (McGuinness 1996), and the work of bringing the application of its principles into domestic, legal and constitutional frameworks will continue to be a challenge for the future (McGuinness 1996).

As discussed earlier in this chapter, the broadening of the scope of behaviours considered to be possibly abusive has dramatically increased since the 1960s. This has resulted in the increased reporting of allegations of abuse, an increase in procedures to follow and a rise in information to collect. This expansion of ideas and work is referred to in the literature as 'diagnostic inflation' (Dingwall 1989: 28). The management of the debates generated by this inflationary process now occupies a central role in the child protection discourse and the true extent of the problem remains unknown (Reder *et al.* 1993; King 1997; Parton *et al.* 1997). Societal regulation of child sexual abuse continues to be an evolving process that inevitably affects the management of the problem. Today's concept of child sexual abuse represents multifaceted discourses about professionalism, legal and political interventions, the rights of children and their families, and gender issues (Parton 1991).

Definitions of child sexual abuse

As with the term 'child abuse', there is no substantive definition for 'child sexual abuse' at the present time (Wattam 1996; Buckley *et al.* 1997; Parton *et al.* 1997;). There is a wide spectrum of behaviours to be considered. These behaviours have been categorized to include incest, paedophilia, molestation, exhibitionism, statutory rape, rape, voyeurism, child prostitution, child pornography and sexual sadism (Kempe and Kempe 1984). There is no general consensus of definition, nor general criteria or guidelines for establishing the existence of child sexual abuse (Finklehor 1986; Parton and Parton 1989; Robin 1991; Cooper 1993). As with child abuse, defining the phenomenon is fraught with value-based and cultural difficulties (Wolfe and Wolfe 1988).

One of the probable reasons why there is no consensus on the definition is that sexual abuse takes a variety of forms, as referred to above. As discussed previously with regard to child abuse in general, there is a commonly used 'umbrella' definition covering the various forms of abuse and referred to as the 'narrow orthodox definition' of child sexual abuse (Archard 1999: 80). This definition, most commonly found in official literature, frequently quoted and used in the *Working Together* document (DHSS 1986; DoH 1999), is the one attributed to Schechter and Roberge (1976). Child sexual abuse is 'the involvement of dependent, developmentally immature children and adolescents in sexual activities that they do not fully comprehend and to which they are unable to give informed consent or that violate the social taboos of family roles' (Schechter and Roberge 1976: 129). This definition adequately covers the broad spectrum of types of child sexual abuse.

An example of the continued search for definitional consensus is demonstrated in Kempe and Kempe's (1984) amalgamation of three definitions of child sexual abuse. First, they refer to Mrazek and Kempe (1981) who have said that child sexual abuse is the sexual use of a child by an adult for his/her own gratification without consideration of the child's psychosocial development. Second, they refer to Mrazek et al.'s (1983) work that describes:

1   the battered child whose injuries are primarily in the genital area;
2   the child who has attempted or experienced actual intercourse or other inappropriate genital contact with an adult; and
3   the child who has been inappropriately involved with an adult in sexual activities not covered by 1 or 2.

Finally, they refer to the National Centre on Child Abuse and Neglect whose definition is: 'contacts or interactions between a child and an adult when the child is being used for sexual stimulation of that adult or another person' (Kempe and Kempe 1984: 10). While these definitions cover a wide range of behaviours thought to be abusive, they do not include many other factors considered to be of significance, such as the age of the child, the context of the harm and the cultural milieu. Further to these might be added the recent rise in computer technology resulting in some paedophiles using internet chatrooms to sexually 'groom' and/or harass vulnerable children.

The search for objective definitions in contemporary discourse appears to be becoming redundant as the emphasis shifts towards a perspective on child sexual abuse that focuses on the individual child's needs within the context in which the harm occurs. In many forms of child abuse and neglect there is seldom any definitive physical or forensic evidence of abuse except in severe cases.

The absence of definitive signs of abuse is nowhere more prevalent than in the case of child sexual abuse. The reliance of basing child protection work and decisions on assessments of risk factors is a contentious activity. There have existed theories of the causality of child sexual abuse that offered definitions that were causally linked to risk factors said to have been identified by research or socially determined. Examples of these are outlined below in order to illustrate some pitfalls associated with such attempts to identify risk.

The influence of special interest groups on definitions of child sexual abuse

A review of the history of the phenomenon of child sexual abuse has revealed a myriad of interested groups involved in the identification and treatment of child sexual abuse. Some of these have been official organizations such as the NSPCC in England and others less formally organized, but equally influential, such as feminist groups. Other influential groups comprise those who have offered explanations with regard to the causes of child sexual abuse, such as the School of Psychoanalysis. These groups have defined child sexual abuse in terms of their own causal theories and have created a maze of different and sometimes contradictory definitions, resulting in an 'understandable malleability' of the term (Archard 1999: 82).

As stated above, there have been a variety of interested groups each offering different definitions of child sexual abuse that reflect the theoretical basis of that particular group. Six perspectives are regularly quoted as having influenced the relationship between definitions and perceived causes of child sexual abuse, and these are identified and discussed below.

The sociological perspective

The first perspective is the sociological perspective. Some writers have suggested that many cases of child sexual abuse are indirectly caused by sociological factors such as the society's philosophy and value system, especially in terms of the prevailing cultural attitudes toward violence. An underlying cumulative stress model suggests that living under difficult economic circumstances and in underprivileged social conditions contributes to the stress and frustration experienced by individuals with dependent offspring. The degree of stress experienced is said to be a determinant of abuse. There is also the theory of a cycle of deprivation that implies that there is a risk of abuse being repeated in successive generations unless the cycle can be broken. Many children are believed to be at risk of sexual abuse if one of their parents was abused, despite there being no sound research to confirm this. Sociological explanations maintain that societal changes in the breakdown of traditional community neighbourhoods, increase in divorce and the resultant withering of family bonds have all led to a social isolation that has left children vulnerable to sexual abuse.

The feminist perspective

The second perspective is a feminist one. Reid (1989) refers to the feminist perspective of child sexual abuse, with its focus on incest, which defines sexual abuse as the abuse of male power in the family. Hallett and

Birchall (1992) quote the Incest Survivors' Campaign definition of child sexual molestation as being abuse performed by any person whom that child sees as a figure of authority and respect. In both these definitions, sexual abuse is seen as the abuse of *power*. Child sexual abuse is seen to be the product of a patriarchal social structure and male socialization. While the inclusion of the misuse of power ultimately may form part of a substantive definition, the introduction of the term 'incest' does not appear to enhance the move towards a consensus definition of child sexual abuse. This is because the term 'incest' has no consensual definition, and is used to cover a whole gamut of sexual transgressions perpetrated on a child by a member of that child's family or surrogate family (Birchall 1989; Howitt 1992).

The systems perspective

A third perspective is provided by Family Systems Theory (Satir 1967; Minuchin and Fishman 1981). Here child sexual abuse is viewed as a symptom of a dysfunctional family system. Examples may be where a mother has had to take work in the evenings to support the family, or where there is a child with learning difficulties or physical disability. In either case, the frustrations resulting from having to cope with what seem to be insurmountable problems place undue stress on the whole family system. This stance holds that both parents are responsible for their role in the sexual abuse. Feminism has challenged this position as being a deflection of responsibility for abuse from the perpetrator.

The public health perspective

The fourth perspective is the 'disease model' of child sexual abuse, also called the 'public health model' by Parton (1985). This model is represented by the medical/scientific perspective. The perspective holds the assumption that as research has identified what the nature of child sexual abuse is, it can equally identify the perpetrators and victims of such abuse. Parton *et al.* (1997) state that this model, as originally conceived in the 1960s, claims that scientific and objective knowledge will allow professionals to identify abuse and intervene benignly on behalf of children.

The psychiatric perspective

Another orientation written within the disease model is represented in psychiatry, where the perpetrator is known to have an individual psychopathology with a diagnosed mental disorder. The assumption is that the perpetrator is not wholly responsible for the harm caused and is in need of psychiatric treatment. Under this psychiatric perspective the victim would also be considered to be in need of psychiatric or psychological treatment. The psychoanalytic model promulgated by Freud that continues to be adopted by the present-day school of psychoanalysis and often regards a patient's current psychological distress as a symptom of repressed sexual abuse in childhood would also come under this psychiatric perspective. Recovered Memory Syndrome and the False Memory Syndrome, discussed earlier, are examples of current dilemmas that reflect the problems related to the employment of the Freudian interpretation of child sexual abuse.

Attempts have been made to identify a profile of a typical adult offender using research studies. Such traits as poor impulse control, low self-esteem, external locus of control and other antisocial behaviours have been suggested. Lists of risk assessment categories have been assembled involving the perpetrators as well as the likely victims. However, none of these has been reliably identified in the research as having predictive value (Parton *et al.* 1997).

The interactionist perspective

It is beginning to be accepted that a social interactionist perspective of child sexual abuse which moves away from an emphasis on individual pathology is to be preferred (Parton *et al.* 1997). Practitioners should be able to reflexively integrate a multitude of factors such as sociological, psychological, economic and environmental, as they all have a part to play in the phenomenon of child sexual abuse. The establishment of a therapeutic relationship between client and practitioner is the first priority in ensuring that accurate information is obtained. Thereafter, the cooperation of participants in the multidisciplinary network to share information in the assessment and management of child sexual abuse will be required. Individual relationships and respect are needed at each of these stages and are enhanced in a well-organized and supportive milieu for practitioners and clients alike. In addition, there is a need for clarification of the lines of communication between agencies for the enhancement of these relations (Birchall and Hallett 1995). The challenge is for professionals from different agencies to be committed to the multidisciplinary method of working.

It can be appreciated that the above perspectives have come to represent a maze of definitions in respect of the phenomenon of child sexual abuse. Some of them have been applied with 'messianic zeal' (Stevenson 1989b) and were exercised at the cost of clients who were sometimes forced into positions to fit the theory. Nevertheless, some of these perspectives are accurate and worthy of consideration. However, as child sexual abuse is complex and the result of multiple causes, it is highly unlikely that there will ever be a definitive definition that is all-embracing.

Incidence and prevalence of child sexual abuse

There is widespread agreement that incidence and prevalence statistics are unreliable (Finklehor 1986; Anthony *et al.* 1988; O'Hagan 1989; Reid 1989; Howitt 1992; Parton *et al.* 1997). As with the problems of defining child sexual abuse, as discussed above, it is rare to find precise definitions of the terms 'incidence' and 'prevalence'. In fact, both terms are often used interchangeably in the literature as if meaning the same thing. Even when a definition is made in a study, the extent of child sexual abuse can still only be discussed in terms of rough estimations. The reason for this is that research literature that attempts to give us the size of the problem is fraught with difficulties that have to do with significant variations of survey techniques and different definitions of child sexual abuse. For instance, it is not uncommon for different methodologies and sampling procedures to be employed in the compilation of statistics (Finklehor 1986; Anthony *et al.* 1988).

All of these factors combined make it difficult to compare the findings of various studies and to generalize from them. As a result, it is quite possible that there is a vast array of child sexual abuse cases that are not included in certain study samples. Researchers often ignore some cases that other research workers with different definitions would include in their sample. In fact, the literature reflects a snowballing effect, as one can see where dozens of unrelated research attempts to establish prevalence figures have resulted in creating even greater variety of outcomes (O'Hagan 1989).

Before discussing the 'rough estimations' in regard to the occurrence of child sexual abuse, it is worth examining some of the issues surrounding incidence and prevalence studies in order to more fully appreciate the scope and the extent of the complexities of research in this area. First, it is necessary to define what we mean by incidence and prevalence studies. Second, it is important to know the major variations found in both of these types of study. Thereafter, the implications of these studies and their epidemiological value will be discussed. Finally, some current research figures will be quoted to establish the approximate size of the problem.

Defining incidence and prevalence

Much of the literature referring to the extent of child sexual abuse uses the terms 'incidence' and 'prevalence' without specifically defining them. More often, studies refer to their identified sample in descriptive terms. A clearer distinction between incidence and prevalence is needed. The *Concise Oxford Dictionary* defines 'incidence' as, 'falling on or contact with a thing; manner or range of occurrence or action...; range, scope or extent of influence...'. The same dictionary defines 'prevalence' as 'generally existing or occurring'. It would seem from these brief definitions that 'incidence' has more specificity than 'prevalence'. Incidence studies could be defined as those exploring the characteristics and number of officially reported cases of child sexual abuse.

One of the only studies to specify a definition of 'incidence' was that by Finklehor and Hotaling (1984). In this study they assert that a true *incidence* study would tell us how many new cases of child sexual abuse occurred each year. 'Prevalence' studies, on the other hand, are those generally accepted as surveys and are based on retrospective, self-reports from selected samples (O'Hagan 1989). It is suggested that this specification and distinction between the two report styles is useful in order to maintain a clear understanding of what their numbers are representing. Incidence studies refer to those cases that have come to the knowledge of the authorities. Prevalence studies may include cases that were never reported to officials as well as reported cases. It is important to recognize this distinction as the two sets of figures are often widely different (Finklehor and Hotaling 1984; Howitt 1992). Despite this difference, both sets of figures should be viewed as important in attempting to come to an understanding of the phenomenon of child sexual abuse.

Difficulties in the interpretation of incidence and prevalence studies

The variations among incidence studies are abundant. There are inconsistencies in definitions of the nature of the abuse, which are the perpetrators of that abuse, the age of the victim and sampling procedures. In addition, each of these areas presents its own set of variables. For example, is the age of the child recorded at the onset of the problem or at the time of disclosure to the authorities, and does the recorded data that lists both male and female as perpetrators offer specificity as to the primary perpetrator (Finklehor and Hotaling 1984; Finklehor 1993). It might be assumed that discovering the frequency of child sexual abuse would be one of the simpler tasks facing the social scientist (Howitt 1992). However, not only is it extremely difficult to get a clear picture of the extent and nature of child sexual abuse from publications, it is also difficult to get a precise idea of the identity of the abusers.

One of the major criticisms of incidence reports has been that those who base their conclusions only on reported cases seriously underestimate the problem (Kempe and Kempe 1978; Finklehor and Hotaling 1984; Reid 1989). The failure to report cases of sexual abuse to child protection agencies by many professionals is well proven in the literature (Finklehor and Hotaling 1984; Powell 1991; Robin 1991). In addition, there are those cases known only to those who are involved and no disclosure is ever made. In both of these instances there is no clear or commonly shared explanation expressed in the literature to say why some cases are reported and some are not.

Another criticism, or source of variation, found in incidence reports is the large number of unsubstantiated reports that become part of the statistics. Such unfounded reports are most often the result of insufficient legal evidence (Powell 1991; Wattam 1992). Finally, 'false allegations', as discussed by Reid (1989), Robin (1991), Wattam (1992) and Parton *et al.* (1997), point to an area that is acknowledged as time-consuming and exacting for professionals, children and those adults involved in the allegations. At this time there are no criteria that would allow expressions of concern or allegations of suspected child sexual abuse to be dismissed out of hand. It has been said that 'two beliefs – that all sexual contact between an adult and a child can be serious and that sexual abuse is difficult to detect – underpin child protection practice' (Parton *et al.* 1997: 190).

In practice, it may only be possible to determine whether an allegation is true or false after a professional review. This area of professional concern has been addressed by many studies (e.g. Faller 1985; Risin and McNamara 1989; Kalichman *et al.* 1990; Amphlett 1992; Evans and Miller 1992; Hutchison 1993; Reder *et al.* 1993; Lindsey 1994; Parton *et al.* 1997). Both Reid and Robin remind us that children are victimized when they have been sexually abused or when they have been victims of a false allegation.

All unsubstantiated reports and false allegations require professional skill and the expertise of staff qualified in matters of child abuse. This management requires full multiagency planning, provision and sensitivity in order to resolve a situation successfully. The results of a study by Thorpe (1994) indicated that from the total sample of child abuse referrals investigated in Western Australia, 49 per cent of children were considered to be abused or at risk of abuse or neglect. This would leave 51 per cent as unsubstantiated allegations not included in the official statistics, despite the fact that they formed approximately half the practitioners' workload. Statistics need to be kept of false allegations and unsubstantiated cases as these represent the outcome of detailed investigations. The omission of unsubstantiated cases raises a second issue regarding the numbers of children who may still be in need of help but who do not officially qualify for assistance. Many of these children may well be in need of some positive intervention in other directions.

The epidemiological value of incidence and prevalence studies

The available evidence supports O'Hagan's (1989) assertion that research studies concerning the prevalence of child sexual abuse are misleading in their statistics and have assumed an authority and status wholly incompatible with their real worth. According to O'Hagen, the major contribution of prevalence figures has been political. Their use has served to intensify the public's abhorrence of child sexual abuse, thereby making it more difficult for people to accept the need for developing alternative, non-punitive strategies for dealing with the problem. Kaul (1983) agrees that epidemiological figures have often aroused community indignation in that they so often blame parents for what are described as callous, wilful and irresponsible acts.

However, Kaul (1983) and Finklehor (1993) would argue that the collating of such statistics is necessary for their preventative value. It is hoped that sufficient knowledge of the problem will be gained to be able to develop policy and educational principles to change those characteristics conducive to abuse. Although clearly of some value for the planning of services and for the overall demographic picture of victims and perpetrators, the question remains as to how far this kind of information is of specific value for the practitioner managing an individual case. While it is useful for a practitioner to have a general overall picture of the problem, each case always requires individual consideration.

The major contribution of statistical findings for practitioners relates to the fact that there are no epidemiological markers that can readily lead a clinician to *exclude* the possibility of sexual abuse. The significant finding is that the prevalence of sexual abuse is widespread and that in no subgroup is it clearly absent or rare (Finklehor 1993). Several investigations have identified common marital and family patterns, and behaviours of abused children. These investigations have also emphasized that the risk factors do not imply that the non-abusive family members have partly been responsible for the abuse, and nor have they helped clinicians to determine that abuse has occurred in a particular instance (Powell 1991). The mere *presence* of risk factors in themselves do *not* mean that abuse has occurred or is likely to occur.

Incidence/prevalence studies give us correlations, not causation. Risk factors revealed by correlation studies may form part of a differential diagnosis of possible child abuse and may need to be excluded. The unit of study in epidemiology is the group rather than the individual. Risk factors, therefore, are more useful as a guide to prevention than as tools that can be used in the actual detection of abuse (Finklehor 1993). The extent to which classic risk factors are associated with child sexual abuse cannot be determined without comparisons between a broad sample of individuals who have sought clinical treatment, and individuals from the general population who have not sought clinical help. However, it should also be acknowledged that classic studies of incidence and prevalence all suggest and point the way to further refinements and new, better methodologies for the future (Kaul 1983; Mrazek *et al.* 1983; Powell 1991; Finklehor 1993).

An understanding of these criticisms of incidence studies needs to be acknowledged and taken into account by those who are engaged in collecting statistics. It needs to be stressed that the numbers that have been collected are representative of trends and are not meant to be definitive statements of occurrence of sexual abuse in any particular community (Finklehor 1982; Mrazek *et al.* 1983; Finklehor and Hotaling 1984; ACCCA 1989, 1992; Vizard *et al.* 1995). Considering the present lack of consensus over definitions and methods of recording, perhaps it will not be possible to obtain reliable statistics in this difficult area.

However, even limited statistics have value in their ability to demonstrate the workload of agencies. They also have value in that they provide information such as the ages and gender of children being referred as well as a profile of offenders. The specific information that such studies generate can be used to plan and improve services for children, their families and communities in general. The compilation, display and discussion of these statistics is also valuable as feedback to practitioners, as a motivational aid to morale and as an enhancement of their confidence.

Statistical estimations of incidence and prevalence

Despite the aforementioned criticisms of incidence/prevalence studies, the pervasiveness of the problem of child sexual abuse is demonstrated in a number of studies. American statistics quote 1 in 4 girls and 1 in 10 boys who will experience some form of unwanted sexual activity before the age of 18 years (Howitt 1992; Finklehor 1993). Many of the early classic incidence and prevalence studies came from America and for that reason are quoted here as they have provided the backdrop from which others have evolved.

One of these classic studies is the National Incidence Study of Child Abuse and Neglect which Finklehor and Hotaling (1984) appraised. This study gave estimations of how many cases of child abuse and neglect were known to professionals in the USA during a one-year period. A stratified random sample representative of the whole country provided the information. Thereafter, using an elaborate system of weightings to extrapolate from case studies the investigators arrived at the figure of 44,700 cases of sexual abuse known to professionals for the year May 1979 to April 1980. One of the major drawbacks to this study was the fact that their definition of child abuse was limited to parents and caregivers, and if sexual abuse is limited to this kind of restriction then a large proportion of the population is automatically excluded.

Mrazek *et al.* (1983) conducted a study to determine the frequency and nature of child sexual abuse in the UK. The figures that were projected from this study were again compiled on the basis of cases reported to professionals. The incidence rate reported was of about 1 in 6000 children per year and in the order of 3 in 1000 during childhood.

The Mrazek *et al.* (1983) study pointed to another commonly shared outcome in that they found 74 per cent of the perpetrators were known to the child. Russell (1983), in her American study, found that 11 per cent of perpetrators were strangers, 61 per cent were known but unrelated and 30 per cent were relatives. Finklehor (1993) has quoted prevalence rates in community studies that range from 6 to 62 per cent for females and 3 to 16 per cent for males. In this same work, Finklehor goes on to say that the mean ratio across eight epidemiological studies is 2.5 girls for every boy or an expectation that 29 per cent of victims are male; a discrepancy that is less than once thought.

The above estimations roughly represent the order of magnitude of abuse that professionals are likely to encounter and for which local authorities should seek to make provision. Even though it is not possible to obtain precise statistics, it can still be appreciated that a vast number of different professionals will need to cooperate in this area. Whatever the size of the problem, the efficient operation of these services depends to a large degree on the quality of interagency coordination and collaboration among the professionals involved.

The overall impact of incidence and prevalence figures indicates that child sexual abuse is a major social problem. The reasons why abuse has come so strongly into public awareness and caused a 'moral panic', with attendant demands for something to be done, lie in an understanding of contemporary social, legal, economic and political discourses in relation to the contemporary social constructions of childhood and the evolution of the child protection discourse. These issues will be examined in the next two chapters.

Summary

Child abuse and child sexual abuse have been known throughout history, but it is only in recent times that they have become a matter of public concern. It was not until the early 1960s that child abuse was established as being of professional socio-medical concern. Following the lead of Kempe and his associates, the identification and management of child abuse became a matter of social concern that was based upon a public health model of detection, diagnosis and treatment. Thereafter, the definition of child abuse broadened to include a greater range of harmful events experienced by children. The lack of a consensual definition of child abuse allowed for a malleability of the term and its use for many different and often exaggerated purposes. The cultural and societal relativity of child abuse led the way to its definition as an evolving social construction. Reification of the terms of abuse occurred and the use of an orthodox, 'umbrella' definition of abuse was advocated by many authorities. Defining the social construction of child abuse and achieving the balance between prevention, investigation and treatment to achieve a comprehensive welfare paradigm continues to be challenging for child welfare work in the contemporary world.

Social, political and economic changes that have occurred in society since the 1950s contributed to a redefinition of child sexual abuse as a social problem that demanded action. In particular, the existence of conflicting and competing definitions based upon various causal theories of child sexual abuse, pursued by different interest groups, complicated the management of the problem for clients and practitioners. While in theory, the positivistic paradigm was originally considered to be the best way to identify and treat cases of abuse, this was often of little practical value due to the complex and often ambiguous nature of the phenomenon. Research attempted to identify personal and environmental circumstances associated with known cases of child sexual abuse in order to predict and prevent the phenomenon. Unfortunately, the available evidence revealed a low correlation between these factors, so making such predictions unreliable. Using this approach revealed a great number of false positives.

Incidence and prevalence studies in relation to child sexual abuse all reflect the lack of a consensual definition. As a result, confusion exists in respect of the size of the problem. Adding to the confusion is the fact that unsubstantiated abuse referrals are often omitted from the official statistics. Unfortunately, it seems that the lack of comprehensive statistics remains a fact in most countries. Nonetheless, epidemiological studies have confirmed that the occurrence of child sexual abuse is widespread.

2 The evolving social construction of childhood

Introduction

The evolution of the social construction of child abuse led to a significant number of definitional problems. It is not surprising, therefore, that at the conceptual and theoretical levels even more fundamental problems and criticisms are evident. Initial attempts to protect children from abuse revealed the contradictory nature of underlying discourses about the nature of childhood itself.

The positivistic approach of scientific psychology has dominated sociological discourses and initially provided the major framework for assessment in child protection work. Recently, doubts have been cast upon this approach. The sociological identification of children as a social group worthy of study in its own right has gradually gained recognition. This recognition is paralleled with the contemporary sociological interest in the body as a subject in its own right. This has been accompanied by a shift away from the objectivistic paradigm in the child protection discourse. This move to a more subjectivist paradigm will be illustrated through a discussion of significant stages in the periodization of childhood, as it is now recognized that the concept of childhood is an evolving social construction. The changing categorization of children and the evolving child-adult relationship has consequences for practice. This will be explored in terms of the scientifically measured child, the child in the consumer culture and the welfare child. This will be followed by a discussion of the theoretical and practical concerns regarding the concepts of childhood innocence, social anxiety, protectionism and 'children's rights'.

Constructions of childhood

Childhood is now generally perceived to be a social and historical construction that is generated and maintained by the cultural milieu in which it is situated (James and Prout 1990). Therefore, childhood is a collective abstraction that has been ascribed a specific social status delineated by boundaries that vary over time and relate to a particular cultural setting (Jenks 1996; King 1997, 1999; Parton *et al.* 1997). Childhood is not a fixed construct and can never be entirely separated from other variables such as age, class, gender or ethnicity (Franklyn 1995b). While biological immaturity in childhood is a fact of life, the way that this immaturity is understood and made meaningful is a fact of culture (James and Prout 1990).

Childhood is a construct that has varied over historical periods in different cultures, as well as in different social groups. Its meaning is in a constant state of flux and is the subject of debate, not only within the intimacy of the family, but also in the broader social institutions of society. Politics, education, law, health and the media all have defined responsibilities and rules for children. One problem for contemporary society is that children will continually contest the boundaries as set by adults. Thus, childhood in this sense can be defined at any one time not only by its *separation* from adulthood, but also, through the degree of its *exclusion* from adulthood (Buckingham 2000).

Sociological construction of childhood

Sociology originally neglected the study of childhood (Mayall 1996). It was considered to be the province of psychology, particularly developmental psychology. Childhood was considered by the developmental psychologists to be a biological process in which the child passed through various stages of emotional, social, cognitive and physical development. Underpinning this was the positivistic view of the child as an object for study and as such the child was perceived to be a passive agent in the process.

In so far as traditional sociology had acknowledged childhood, it had subsumed the child under the context of the family. Similarly, until recently, sociology also included children under the institution of education (Mayall 1996). Moreover, childhood was not perceived to be a construction in its own right, but one constructed by adults. It is only in more recent times that it has been advocated that childhood be recognized as an identifiable category separate from the constructions of the family and education.

With the recognition of childhood as a social construction, the influences of the wider social contexts of age, gender, ethnicity and class began to be acknowledged (James and Prout 1990). In addition, the impact on childhood of the economic and political forces of the day also need to be considered in the construction of childhood. At a macro level, children's lives are structured and regulated by the adult division of labour at home and in schools. At the micro level, the early learning of appropriate social, emotional and physical behaviour, as well as encouragement to cognitive development in the family environment, contribute to the construction of childhood.

Sociology of the body

The growing awareness of the construction of childhood is paralleled in the sociological literature with an increase in academic interest in the regulation of bodies. At one time, it had even been suggested that the body should serve as the organizing principle for sociology (Shilling 1993; Turner 1994). Shilling has said that the body's 'absent presence' in classical sociology can be traced to the foundation and development of the discipline. As referred to earlier, the sociology of childhood had been absent from traditional sociology, although it was sometimes referred to in terms of its 'future' value but had no current status in its own right. As James and Prout (1990) have concluded, reference to childhood has been more often conceived of in terms of its romantic past or in terms of the future worth of the child as a competent citizen in society.

Shilling presents four major social factors that have formed the context for the relatively recent rise in the interest in the 'body' in sociology. These are the growth of 'second wave' feminism in the 1960s; demographic changes that have focused attention on the needs of older people in western societies; the rise of consumer culture linked to modern capitalism; and the growing crisis in our knowledge of the regulation of bodies. The heightened awareness of the problem of child sexual abuse, childhood as a social construction and the rights of children have been propelled by some of these same social factors.

The contemporary interest in the sociology of the body can be seen as part of a more general movement in the social sciences which has attempted to come to terms with the embodiment of the human actor, and hence with the relationships between emotionality and feeling in relation to purposeful activity (Turner 1994). Since the eighteenth century, naturalistic views of the body have exerted considerable influence on how people have perceived the relationship between the body, self-identity and society (Parton 1985; Bourdieu 1993; Shilling 1993).

The process of the development of self-identity in childhood can be observed in its initial stages as the integration of the influences of the family, and then further through the integration of the wider social context of society in general. Children learn at home, through rewards for appropriate behaviour, that physical and mental well-being are interrelated. The situation is reversed when the child enters school, where cognitive behaviour is given priority over the body. The subjugation of bodily needs is considered necessary for learning to take place. Traditionally therefore, adults have perceived children as products to be controlled and moulded according to the values and moralities of the adults. In this sense, the view that adults have of children is said to be 'adultcentric' (Parton *et al.* 1997). In the process, adults define what it means to be a 'child' (Buckingham 2000).

The current social order that has supported the adultcentric view is now challenged (Mayall 1996). Children are no longer viewed as totally passive agents and, in fact, are actively encouraged to have a voice in contemporary society. Authority in general is in question. Several factors in society are likely to be responsible for this, including the influence of the feminist movement that has challenged society's traditional power structure and its mainly male-dominated social order.

Capabilities and constraints placed upon 'bodies' define individuals and generate the social, political and economic relations that characterized national attitudes. Individuals in the late twentieth century sought to define their bodies as individual possessions, integrally related to their self-identities (Frank 1993; Shilling 1993).

At the macro level, the sociology of the body has particular relevance to the social construction of childhood, as in the production of physical and social capital (Bourdieu 1993). At this level, parents and teachers demonstrate to children that their bodies have value in countless ways. Through their social and physical interactions with children they impose constructs in terms of ethnicity, gender, status, age and a host of other related moral, social, health and leisure expectations.

Bourdieu's interest in the body derives from the theory of social reproduction and the means by which 'cultural capital' is accumulated and maintained in a certain social strata (Shilling 1993). As such, Bourdieu has examined the multiple ways in which the body as a social and biological phenomenon has been commodified. According to Bourdieu's work, different social classes develop varying ideals of body image. The richer dominant classes are said to have more leisure time and greater health opportunities to develop a body that reflects recommended ideals. These 'symbolic' values can be converted into social and cultural capital – for example, rules of etiquette at sporting clubs (Shilling 1993). In these terms, it is in the family and in the school that the symbolic values are first ascribed to children and form the basis of an embodiment of the child although they are influenced by the overarching norms of society in which the family is located.

The varying experiences that constitute the embodied child as a person invoke a paradox as they are based on adult notions of what they consider to be appropriate ideas of child development. This process often excludes the voice of the child. Power relationships with adults limit children's opportunities and their abilities to find 'place and space' for their embodied selves (Mayall 1996). There is a need to reconsider the social and political status of childhood, especially the manner of its social construction in terms of time and place.

In order to improve the general welfare of children it is important to include them in the political agenda. There is a parallel here in the struggle for the recognition of feminism as a sociological perspective and the way that women's issues have since become placed on the political agenda. It is necessary for sociology to recognize childhood as a distinct sociological category. As asserted in the Cleveland Report, Butler-Sloss has stated that children have been seen as objects of concern, but not as people who clearly have rights as citizens. Nevertheless, the 'voice' of the child remains silent in many current child protection practices.

As described above, the sociology of childhood is now recognized as a unique area of study in it own right. In order to understand how the social construct of childhood has developed over time, an overview of the periodization of childhood now follows.

Periodization of childhood

There have been significant changes historically in the roles and attitudes toward children and the way that these changes have been periodized. From the earliest writings of Socrates, childhood constructions and a vision of the child have been consistent with the mores of the day (Jenks 1996; Corby 2000). Even before the advent of widespread literacy, Plato's *Republic* contained descriptions of stories to which children should and should not be exposed (Lee 1958; Buckingham 2000). Despite this early interest in the child, as pointed out by Philippe Ariès (1962), the concept of childhood as distinct from the adult state did not exist until after the Middle Ages. However, as Buckingham (2000) points out, there had been many representations of adult ideas about childhood, as depicted, for example, in medieval paintings and also in the later Rennaissance period.

In the Middle Ages children were regarded as small adults. Accordingly, they were ascribed a life of work, play and responsibility. Once physically able, around the age of 5 or 6, children went straight into the community as part of the labour force. At this time, work and home life were not sharply divided (Parton 1985). Family bonds within particular communities were strong due to the social isolation and lack of mobility in agrarian societies. Such societies typified *Gemeinschaft,* a term introduced by the German historian Tónnies, to denote the sacred society wherein the blood ties of kinship bonds are not destroyed with stratification (Becker and Barnes 1961). Kinship bonds helped to establish status and a shared homogeneity.

The collective fellowship of this society prized equivalence and as such individuality was not a well-recognized concept. Being dependent on the land for survival, people were close to nature and their lives structured around the seasons. Functional/reciprocal relationships existed between adults and children. The children were seen as resources for the continual protection of the adults' territory and for labour in the fields. In this labour-intensive economy, with the need for the community to protect their holdings, physical strength was valued. Children were also a valued resource in the reinforcement and extension of communities and their wealth. For example, they could be offered in marriage to establish and strengthen social and economic bonds with neighbouring clans, cemented by the exchange of dowries and/or payments made to the grooms. Such arrangements extended the kin network as a resource as well as strengthening social alliances.

Kinship bonds were weakened with the advent of urbanization and the pull toward the cities. The breakdown of primary, sacred societies into secular ones also accompanied the shift to *Gesellschaft*. Tónnies used this term to represent a society characterized by artificial associations of people. That is, a society where associative social bonds were formally structured, in contrast to the informal community kinship bonds of *Gemeinschaft*. The communal nature of society in pre-industrial England was greatly eroded by the division of labour that came with industrialization and separated kinship groups. Jenks (1996) refers to the construction of human *relationality*, the architecture of the nuclear family, as a recognizable complement to the division of labour through industrialization. In other words, the highly cohesive nature of rural communities began to break up as groups and individuals moved to urban centres for work.

During this period of transition from an agrarian to a more urbanized society, children were still expected to work as soon as they were able to do so. Where this was not possible, they were left to their own devices and eventually began to be recognized as troublesome to adults and in need of regulation. It was during this period that children were subjected to exploitation and maltreatment, either working in factories or living on the streets.

In the same period, with the aftermath of the French Revolution, the Age of Enlightenment saw poets of the day romanticizing childhood. For example, one of this period's foremost writers, Rousseau, in *Émile* (1762), promulgated the notion of 'childhood innocence', which was fundamentally different from the state of adulthood (Becker and Barnes 1961; Jenks 1996). Children were perceived as having their own nature, not as 'miniature adults'. They 'arrived' in a primal condition, embodied the 'good' and needed to be educated along natural principles. These notions, based upon the liberated child of nature, sharply clashed with the reality of oppressed child labour in factories and the negative experiences of precocious juvenile delinquents who needed regulation.

In England during the 1840s, various pieces of legislation and parliamentary reports were designed to restrict and improve conditions for children in employment (Parton 1985), the Factory Act 1846 being one such example. The eighteenth-century construction of childhood emerged fragmented and equivocal; torn between notions of innocence and a 'sinful' pessimism born of Evangelical and political anxieties (Hendrick 1990). The concept of childhood as comprising sweetness and innocence was being challenged by the notion of children as carriers of original sin and in need of strict socialization.

During this period, the social structure of the day had legitimated in law the subordination of children to the power of parents, especially fathers, in accordance with the patriarchal attitudes that predominated in the eighteenth century (May 1978; Parton 1985; James and Prout 1990; Jenks 1996). Parton (1985: 27) refers to the work of May (1978), who commented on the situation of children at that time, stating 'there was a universal belief in the sanctity of parental rights including the use of chastisement so that physical punishment was part of the normal experience of most children'.

During the eighteenth century, children were involved in employment and were viewed as an economic commodity. Most commonly, they were viewed as the *property of their parents* (May 1978; Parton 1985). Their social control was left to the parents, but there arose the problem of what to do with 'wayward', homeless or abandoned children, for whom strict regulation was thought to be necessary, as they were regarded as delinquents in society. Because the family did not provide this regulation these children were placed in reformatories run by the state. Children, in general, were seen to be in need of protection as well as reforming, and the growing popularity of school as a means of social control for the majority of children to some extent assisted in this. In the 1830s and 1840s, criminologists felt that education would prevent children from the poorer sectors of society from reproducing and taking over (Hendrick 1990).

The scientific study of children, with a firm empirical basis, was initiated in 1840 when Charles Darwin began a record of the growth and development of his own children (Morss 1990). This notion of development resonated with modernity and the stress on growth and progress. The scientific rationalist approach now exerted its influence on social thinking. The Darwinian framework positioned development as necessary and inevitable for the progress of humanity. Thus, Darwin was one of the most influential sources of ideas for theories of child development, and introduced the beginnings of the new science of developmental psychology (Morss 1990; Archard 1993).

Following the work of Darwin, the growth of schools for children in the last quarter of the nineteenth century played a central role in the beginning of a new construction of childhood. Despite the obvious benefits to the welfare of the child, the introduction of schools served to reinforce the child's dependence on adults and, as pointed out by Hendrick (1990), also reduced children's sense of their own value. Where previously they had been included in the labour force, and so could make a significant contribution to the family, they were now economically marginalized. Children were still not being recognized as a distinct social group with a voice of its own.

As the nineteenth century drew to a close, the regulatory power of educational authorities imposed itself on both parents and children for compulsory school attendance (Hendrick 1990). Hendrick (1990: 49) refers to the construction of the 'welfare child' during this period when several welfare schemes were introduced with the aim of preventing child cruelty and neglect. The Prevention of Cruelty to Children Act of 1904 introduced the power of the state in the form of local authority powers to remove children and prosecute 'disreputable' parents (Parton 1985: 37). Thereafter, the Children Act of 1908 was instrumental in ensuring the physical care and nurturing of infants as well as introducing formal school medical examinations. Thus, by the beginning of the twentieth century, a new construction of childhood had emerged with children beginning to be seen to have rights independent from adults. However, children were still not being given their own voice, and although interventions were said to be carried out in the 'child's best interests', it was the adults who decided what these 'interests' were (Parton 1985).

At the beginning of the twentieth century, schools were said to have become the human science laboratory for the scientific survey of entire childhood populations. Criminologists, medical specialists, educationalists and psychologists combined to develop the field of empirical research into what was to become the field of child psychology. The focus was on understanding the child socially, educationally and medically, and this saw the beginning of the psycho-medical construction of childhood that led to the psychological study of child development. The result was a proliferation of literature on 'normative' standards, such as the measuring of intelligence, textbooks on educating children and manuals for the parenting of children, much of which has continued to the present day.

One of the major criticisms of the early developmental psychologists was their neglect of children as capable of self-conscious activity (Denzin 1977). They regarded children as passive creatures who could be controlled and conditioned, when in fact later research supported the view that children were capable of reflection and interactive learning. Children were not merely objects waiting to be socialized, but were seen to develop mainly through a process of interaction with adults (Mayall 1996). The symbolic interactionists, among whom Mead (1934) was particularly influential, illustrated how this interactive learning occurred. The development of self-image in children is one example of this. The theory of the self-image of the child followed the tradition of the symbolic interactionists, as depicted in the 'Looking Glass' theory of the development of the self (Cooley 1912; Mead 1934). This early influence recognized the development of the self-image of the child as a dynamic process of social interaction. Children did not develop in isolation, but were influenced by the larger social context of society as well as the immediate context of the family. This view would contrast with the later behaviourist school of psychology that regarded children's behaviour as formed totally through environmental influences (Skinner 1953).

The school of behaviourism, founded by J. B. Watson (1924), has had a profound influence in psychology generally and, indirectly with variations on behaviourism, it continues to do so in such diverse fields as education and psychotherapy. This scientific behaviourism may have been responsible for the subsequent and temporary neglect of the symbolic interactive process highlighted by Cooley and Mead, as referred to above. For Skinner (1953), a chief exponent of behaviourism, the child's personality was formed through a series of conditioned responses. This was a mechanical process of the conditioning of the child's behaviour through rewards and punishments. The strict behaviourist standpoint was later modified by the social learning theorists such as Bandura (1986). These theorists also viewed the personality of the child as a learned phenomenon, but with emphasis on learning, primarily through a modelling of behaviour on significant others.

In marked contrast to the behaviourist view, later theorists, such as Piaget (1974) and Erikson (1963), following on from the earlier writers like Darwin and Freud, viewed the child as developing inevitably through a series of stages. Piaget's theories of cognitive stages have had a profound effect on the study of child development, particularly as it seems that childhood is so often expressed in terms of children's competence and ability. The main feature of developmentalist theories, however, was their emphasis on inherited characteristics and their biological unfolding. This work gave rise to the present view of the psychology of childhood as a product of both environmental and genetic factors. Although developmental psychology has undoubtedly contributed to an understanding of the various stages in child development, by its focus on normative standards it has drawn attention away from the individual child. Also, the social forces that impact on the child, such as the power of adults and the influence on the child of adults' social norms, are neglected. However, the notion of developmental stages continues to exert its influence in child protection work, particularly in reference to medical and educational institutions, where the 'normal' child is the object of study.

Contemporary social constructions of childhood

This section explores more contemporary constructions of childhood, from the 1900s onwards, relating particularly to childhood in western society. It is important to bear this in mind, as children in much of the rest of the world are not regarded according to this conception of childhood.

Numerous events extending over this period in the arenas of politics, economics, sociology, education, health, law, religion and psychology influenced the varying constructions of childhood and the way we treat children. The history of the discourse of childhood can be described as a development from the total ambiguity of the concept of childhood in times past, to contemporary constructions of childhood as a largely unambiguous state, relatively separate from other stages of human development.

James and Prout (1990) usefully summarise the three themes that have predominated in the study of children and childhood over the last century:

1   Ideas of rational development, especially the progression of natural humanity from a savage condition to rational being in theories of evolution. Exemplars of this period of thinking were Rousseau, Auguste Comte and Darwin. Biological and social development were linked and exemplified by Watson, Piaget and Erikson. Children were seen as marginal figures awaiting temporal passage through the acquisition of skills to adulthood. These theorists considered childhood to be a natural stage on the path to becoming an adult.
2   Later theorists accepted an implicit binarism with children being immature, incompetent and in need of socialization, which adults were required to provide.
3   Finally, the concept of childhood began to be seen as a social construct with the definitions of childhood varying not only between cultures but also across time.

It is clear from the above that in the past three centuries perceptions of childhood have undergone many transitions. Hendrick (1990) has commented that the extent to which each fresh construction was a reconstruction is difficult to determine as there appears to be an overlap with each perception. What is clear is that the different constructs have opened the door to different practices in regard to children. Let us examine these in more detail.

The modern child as scientifically measured

The late nineteenth and early twentieth centuries witnessed the development of the positivism in the study and categorization of childhood. Its influence is continued in the contemporary measurement of children's health, personality and ability. For example, in relation to education, norms of appropriate behaviour and expected levels of attainment in school subjects have been established. In addition, parents have been made aware of schools' standards of health and hygiene. The concept of the healthy child is presented to parents as if it is an uncontestable fact, when in practice what is healthy is influenced by a range of social and economic factors, as well as by the interests of the medical profession (Mayall 1996). Epidemiological studies in both England and Australia have shown that standards of health and morbidity for children and adults vary according to levels of poverty, social class and geographical location. These standards are all presented as objective facts, ignoring the 'fact' that notions of ideal health, appropriate behaviour and acceptable norms of educational achievement are all constructed by political and economic factors that are in turn morally constructed by the dominant ideology of the day. In the same way, where normative frameworks are employed, as devised by developmental psychology, there is a tendency to 'blame the victim' who deviates from the norm even though it is only a statistical deviation and their behaviour may not give any cause for serious concern. The dilemma arises from the inappropriate use of a positivistic approach, when intervention in social work cannot be devoid of a value judgement. In child protection, accurate judgements cannot be made without reference to a moral framework.

In the past it was generally believed that our knowledge of the world was based upon valid scientific knowledge. It was felt that people could be held responsible and blamed for tragic events once the objective evidence was obtained. However, contemporary events have called in question so-called objectivity and scientific predictions, particularly with regard to child protection work. The notion of probability in science has emerged and with it the notion of risk. According to Beck (1992), we now live in a 'risk society'. In child protection it is becoming acknowledged that decisions should no longer be made on wholly objective evidence, but within a situated moral, reflexive framework (Parton *et al.* 1997; Parton 1998).

The scientific process of obtaining norms and standards is also being challenged. While this work is described as being 'in the interest of the child', once again it serves to reinforce the construction of the child as a passive agent. Moreover, politics and the law have strengthened the necessity of conformity to these standards by all concerned. Governments and local communities have set up administrative machinery for their implementation. This process does not individualize circumstances and so any deviation from the norm has the tendency to stigmatize a child. School and medical records containing normative data, and the 'labelling' of children are examples of this.

A further example of this process is where a child's misbehaviour is on record and passed on to subsequent teachers with the danger of a self-fulfilling prophesy occurring. Overactive children may well be classified as misbehaving because they do not conform to the school's standards of behaviour. Such children may receive what the school considers to be appropriate sanctions when in fact the child concerned may well have an emotional difficulty and be in need of counselling. The school may be under pressure to produce governmentally required statistics for achievement, as in England where the current 'league tables' compare the achievements of different schools.

Mayall (1996) distinguishes between the 'civilizing' of children and the 'regulation' of children. The early basic civilizing is said to be done in the home, where appropriate behaviour attracts social approval, usually mediated through the emotional relationship that the child has with the parents. Children are taught standards of behaviour devised by the adults so that they are expected, for instance, to feed at particular times, to go to bed at certain times and to achieve standards of hygiene at appropriate times, as in toilet training. In this way, children are regulated by adults with regard to space and chronological time.

At school, the same process can occur, but within a more impersonal relationship. Moreover, the emphasis in schools is on cognitive growth separated from bodily needs, whereas at home a more holistic approach may be experienced by the child. An example of this is the thirsty child being expected to defer gratification until break-time, having been used to immediate satisfaction of thirst. The school reinforces the notion of the child having to conform to the adult agenda and having to unlearn previous behaviour taught in the home. The egocentricity of the child is more accepted at home, but at school once again the child has to conform to the adult agenda where they are rewarded for conforming to the group norm. Perhaps it is in relation to authority that childhood is seen to be at its most passive. Children at school, as well as at home, and in most work situations, are expected to conform to the rules handed down to them by adults as symbols of authority.

The propagation of moral instruction is a major role for most schools. This instruction includes learning the rules of the game in reference to peer group interaction, respect for age-reference groups, ascribed gender role behaviour, individual academic achievement, physical development and acceptance of authority. Durkheim (1961) introduced the notion of schools being the institutions that would teach children the moral and social codes of the wider social community. However, this presents children with a dilemma as the process of learning to conform to the group is usually in conflict with the school's emphasis on individual achievement. The outward symbol of uniformed children is generally heralded as a strategy of increasing group solidarity. This presents another dilemma for children as it means the relative subjugation of their individuality. On the other hand, this learning of the adoption of visible communal signs of the group reinforces the fact that they are part of a larger unit that is being educated for its collective life as future citizens (Durkheim 1961). In this respect each child as a developing adult represents an economic investment in the future of the country as each child's education is financed by the state.

The late/advanced modern child and consumer culture

Since World War II, children have been the focus of concern regarding their vulnerability to the media and their susceptibility to advertizing by commercial organizations. Children have become a distinct consumer group, both directly and indirectly, and material objects have come to contain symbolic value for children. Although children are consumers, they are generally dependent on their parental resources for the purchase of material goods. From personal experience in conducting parent education classes, many parents will agree that up to a certain age they determine the choice of their child's dress. However, once the child develops a body consciousness and becomes influenced by advertising, choice of dress usually is more determined by the child. This is taking place earlier and earlier as the advertising of children's fashion becomes more persistent. There appears to be a movement towards a general consumer empowerment of children throughout childhood as they progress through to the teenage years and thence to adulthood. The concerns expressed about children's vulnerability in this respect are referred to by Buckingham (2000), when he advocates ways of preparing children to deal with the market-place, rather than trying to protect them from it.

The periodization of childhood that occurred after World War II identified 'teenagers' as a separate social group (Giddens 1993). Just as childhood, as a distinct concept, had not been identified as a social entity separate from adulthood, prior to World War II, teenagers had not been considered as a distinct group (Jenks 1996). A significant milestone was the process of formal education that was extended for teenagers and the concept of deferred gratification that was introduced to describe those who stayed on at school (Merton 1963). This sometimes produced conflicts for teenagers in their search for personal freedom and entry into the adult world. The sustained dependency upon adults also had negative economic consequences for parents, apart from the high-income groups who could afford to support their offspring.

The rising markets of capitalistic consumerism during this period quickly perceived a new target group. Teenagers were identified by the term 'adolescence'. This transitory period of hormonal development between childhood and adulthood was targeted by the world markets as a consumer group. At a time of the growing economic prosperity, there was an increase in disposable income and a general optimism that resulted in increased consumer activity. The teenage market was established and reflected in young people's dress, music, leisure activities, cosmetics, films, magazines and other popular media-driven commodities. Despite having been identified as a separate group, most teenagers remained dependent on adults for the satisfaction of basic and commercial needs. The acquisition of material possessions marketed specifically for the teenager was a source of identity, giving some confidence at a time of insecurity in their transition to adulthood.

The transition of the post-industrial economy into the 'age of information' has made knowledge a commodity. It could be argued that during the last two decades there has been a drive for new markets, focusing on children as a target group. In this contemporary construction of childhood, children have become indirect consumers. While they do not have their own disposable income, the media addresses them *as if* they are autonomous in terms of what they will eat, wear, hear, watch and read.

Teenagers and children have been targeted in the information technology boom and are actively involved within the global market-place at home and at school, via television and the internet. Global media communication and participation is increasing for children to a degree that sometimes exceeds their parents' grasp of such rapid developments. Critics of the influences of television and the internet refer to their negative effects on children and teenagers, pointing to the sometimes insidious advertizing employed, as well as the diffusion of what is deemed to be particularly undesirable material. This view of young people's vulnerability fails to acknowledge that for the most part children and teenagers are still dependent upon adults at this stage of their development and so may not necessarily have the freedom of choice that is assumed. On the other hand, it is presumed that parents are sufficiently secure in their relationships with their offspring to be able to regulate their involvement with the media. Some parents are themselves vulnerable to the pressure of the media and come to represent a financial resource to their children, available for their exploitation. In this instance the parent-child relationship can become a dependent one and not a reciprocal one.

The global media culture, represented in particular by the growth of the internet, has accelerated the influence of the 'virtual' world as a means of experiencing action and being. Animated creatures with idealized abilities and physical endowments populate electronic interactive games. Their identity is constructed through images rather than the child's immediate reality. Fears are expressed that children will identify with this similarity or approximation of reality, rather than being actively focused on the here and now.

Concern has been expressed that children's self-image can be harmed by exposure to undesirable models, as well as by giving them a false sense of reality. However, this fear may be groundless, as recent research has suggested that children as young as 6 and 7 can distinguish between fact and fantasy in the visual media (Buckingham 2000). The fear that their identity may be influenced may however have some justification, as children's self-image is partly formed through the process of symbolic interaction (Lawrence 1996). This would also lead us to think that children may not simply be passive recipients of the media, but rather active participants in the process.

Since the work of Bowlby (1969) and Erikson (1963), it has been acknowledged that the quality of the adult-child relationship is a major factor in a child's successful transition to healthy adulthood. However, it seems that children are being encouraged and tempted to spend more time being entertained by their electronic goods and less time in direct contact with their parents. There are reports in the media of parents allowing their children time and access to these worlds of virtual reality as a form of 'in-house' entertainment. This is encouraged as a form of risk management by parents. Some parents feel that by allowing children to play outdoors they are exposing them to possible contact with a dangerous world populated by speeding cars and paedophiles (Buckingham 2000).

Generally, perceived risks in contemporary life often have nothing to do with the actual prevalence of life-threatening dangers (Giddens 1991). People are thought to be in a much safer environment than in previous ages, but despite this parents are actively involved in the purchase of safety apparatus for their children and insurance for themselves against many eventualities in everyday life. Recent medical advances have allowed people to choose the sex of their child and also determine if the child might be at risk of developing certain genetic physical or psychological diseases. Embryos can be genetically analysed and modified to a desired specification. This process of modifying embryos through their collection, storage and manipulation, and selecting one for fertilization is sometimes referred to as having a 'designer child'. This designer child becomes constructed as a medical commodity.

Although some parents are now able to select their child on a scientific basis, this raises moral and even religious questions. One of the questions raised is the morality of choosing a 'perfect' child, bearing in mind that by doing so parents are in effect making a statement about a disability. At this early stage the costs involved prohibit the procedure being widespread and this, in itself, is another issue regarding to whom such procedures are made available. However, and more importantly, should the procedure become widespread it would have serious ramifications for the whole of humankind as it would change the composition of societies. The advancement of technology has created more scope for parents to exercise choice and in so doing attempt to reduce risks. However, the assumption that the world can be the object of precise control in this way is debatable. It is an inescapable observation, however, that parenting by its very nature is a risk occupation.

In the consumer culture, children are seen as the consumers, but it is their parents who often need to make decisions on their behalf. There are centres of entertainment, such as children's sessions at the cinema, where parents will pay for the admission and then leave the children until the performance finishes. Parents have to make an assessment of the degree of risk whenever their children enter a new situation like this, bearing in mind the aim of helping their children develop independence.

The phenomenon of 'parent blaming' when things go wrong can inhibit desires to empower children to take risks as a method of developing independence. Parental decisions of this nature are usually made on an age and ability basis. Parents are faced with a bewildering array of available information to help make these decisions and usually raise the questions of whether the child is old enough, clever enough or mature enough to be allowed to engage in the activity concerned. These three factors of age, ability and maturity are fundamental factors in the social constructions of childhood.

In the late/advanced modern consumer culture, there is another sense in which parents have often been the objects of blame. This is where their children may display what is referred to as 'delinquent behaviour'. Delinquent children are often seen as deviant because their parents are believed not to have exerted sufficient childrearing authority and safeguards. It is often the parent who is blamed for failing to be of sufficient calibre to rear a law-abiding and productive child.

The childhood construction of a 'threat' is not new. The perceived threat of a 'welfare' state is that it reproduces a multigenerational subculture of identifiable groups who have lost basic values with regard to employment, saving and honesty. Entire communities have been pathologized by being stereotyped as representative of the so-called 'yob-culture' (Goldson 1997: 12). Recent medical advances have revealed possible genetic factors claimed to be responsible for deviant behaviour, so absolving some parents from blame. An example of this is a child who exhibits hyperactive behaviour, and is subsequently diagnosed as having attention deficit hyperactivity syndrome (ADHD).

What is described as the new teenage and childhood consumer culture is said to exclude adults in several ways, with the result that children share less time and space with their parents. Perhaps this may not pose a threat, provided parents are more involved in sharing the child's experiences with the television and the internet and balance this with more traditional outdoor activities.

Buckingham (2000) reminds us that the contemporary child has become more critical of adults and is more likely to challenge authority than in past times. Children are increasingly more active and encouraged to express themselves. Some child protection programmes have made children aware that it is their right to say 'no' if an adult asks them to do something that they do not feel is right. They are encouraged by the media to choose their own toys, food, clothes, entertainment and image styles. In this sense they are creating their own identity. This places them in the contradictory position of having to accept parental authority but at the same time claim their freedom.

Parents contribute to this state of confusion by exhorting their children to grow up and behave responsibly, while on the other hand denying them privileges considered appropriate when the child is older. Many parents who attend parent education groups often say that they listen to their children, but seem to be unaware of the need to reflect on the child's feelings and to give them appropriate feedback. Often these parents have to be encouraged to listen actively to their children in this way. In ordinary circumstances it is not uncommon for parents to offer children their advice. Unfortunately, their children become frustrated as they feel their parents are not listening to, nor understanding, them.

A further sense of confusion exists when the media creates 'parallel ideals' (Buckingham 2000: 100) aimed at both children *and* adults. The children depicted in certain 'family' films represent an idealized child that provides a model of aspiration for children and a romantic escape to the past for the parents (Archard 1993). As discussed above, the work of Bourdieu (1993) illustrates how the leisure pursuits of family life translate from economic capital to social capital in these situations. Children, through their engagement in commercial leisure and entertainment facilities, have assumed not only social value for the stratification of society, but also financial value for the economy. Where parents are divorced or separated, a situation is created where many adults seek ready-made sources for eating and entertainment to share with their children during limited access periods. The family has become a leisure opportunity, a unit of consumption. The commercial market continues to play an important role in the construction of the family and in contemporary childhood, placing as it does pressure on parents, particularly where there is a limited income. Attractive goods are regularly displayed and advertized prominently in stores and during children's viewing time on television to tempt children to consume the product. The pressure is increased where the child from a low-income family may be in a school or other peer group setting where others from higher income families are able to purchase more expensive goods. It has been known for children in this situation to become delinquent as they have been unable to resist the temptation to acquire the same goods through theft.

The contemporary welfare child

In western society, it is recognized that the family has the prime responsibility for the welfare of the child although, additionally, the state is also seen to have a collective responsibility in this area. The state is responsible for initiating welfare policy and legislation with a duty to provide finance and support for the implementation of welfare programmes.

At the beginning of the twentieth century, child welfare programmes were originally designed by governments for children who were neglected, abandoned or cruelly treated. Over the next 50 years, specific child protection programmes were relatively nonexistent, but grew from more general child welfare programmes. Since World War II, the notion of child welfare has been extended by various acts of parliament in England and by state laws in Australia, so that legally all children are now included in a child welfare concept that incorporates child protection. The topic of child abuse is now part of the remit of all those who work with children. The contemporary child in a liberal welfare state is one under scrutiny and surveillance (Kempe and Kempe 1978; Dingwall *et al.* 1983; Howitt 1992). This process is also referred to by Leonard (1997) as the metaphor of the 'gaze', a term used to describe the social monitoring of subjects undertaken by the state.

Lindsey (1994) reports that child welfare programmes are designed to make available avenues of opportunity, not just for those identified as abused, but for all children. The balancing of general overall social welfare with the child protection discourse is difficult, as it involves the duty of the state to intervene appropriately in the family while still honouring the rights of children and families to self-determination and independence.

The UK Children Act 1989 states that it is the duty of the state to provide children with the opportunity to achieve satisfactory health and development. A responsibility is also identified for a specific group of children whom the Act (in Section 17) defines as 'in-need'. Local authorities are asked to identify the extent of children in need. Although not expected to meet every individual need, local authorities are responsible for making decisions on service provision. In addition, provision is made in the Act for children who are deemed to be at risk, and for the promotion and safeguarding of their welfare. In Australia, each of the country's six states and two territories has its own Act pertaining to the welfare of children, such as the Child Welfare Act 1989 in Western Australia.

In our contemporary society, the state divides responsibilities for the development and well-being of children between many agencies. As each of the systems involved has its own input, there is a danger that the whole child is sometimes overlooked. It is also unclear how divergent are the views, values and objectives of the various professionals who are the representatives of the respective welfare agencies. On occasion, education, law, medicine and social services may only see a child from the perspective of their particular agency. Efficient interagency coordination and collaboration is essential for the reduction of this well-known separation of a child into diverse categories and the possible neglect of the child's overall needs. The effects of the imminent reorganization of children's services in health, education and social services into one children's trust, as stated in *Every Child Matters* (DfES 2003) in England is eagerly anticipated.

Over the past 100 years, there has been a steady progression from moral campaigners against child cruelty with ensuing legislation on children's welfare rights to more recent laws specifically designed in terms of children's rights, parental responsibilities and the child protection role of the state. Each of these phases has formulated its own perception of the construction of childhood and the role of parents.

Many of our attitudes today still reflect and are influenced by past images of children as innocent and vulnerable, in need of rescuing from 'dangerous' parents and other adults. In her review of the origin of contemporary child protectionists' views, Piper (1999: 35) refers to the 'visible Victorian' child, whose depiction as a weak, sensitive and physically frail individual helped focus philanthropic and state attention on matters of cruelty to children. Piper describes the moral campaigners who sought to rescue children from injustice and cruelty during the Victorian period in England as possessing a sense of religious duty and moral guilt. These traits combined to designate particular forms of maltreatment against children that warranted state sanctions in order to prevent further harm.

Legislation followed that curtailed child employment in certain occupations, such as working in mines, sweeping chimneys and working in factories. Further to this, acts of infanticide, severe chastisement, 'baby farming', abandonment or drunken behaviour by parents were now raised as a matter of public concern and warranted the intervention of child welfare organizations. Many such organizations were from the voluntary sector, and in 1890 a number of them amalgamated to form the NSPCC (Reder *et al.* 1993).

Three major trends relating to adult-child relationships and constructions of childhood continue to exist in contemporary child welfare. The first is that there is a process of monitoring the child as an object of social and scientific review. Underpinning this viewpoint is the positivistic approach that sees the child as a passive object, a developing biological organism, who will proceed through identifiable stages of emotional, cognitive and social immaturity, ultimately to mature as an adult (Erikson 1963; Piaget 1974). The second trend is the role of the moral assessor that has now developed into the role occupied by the 'expert', who employs the findings of research literature as a 'norm' or accepted standard and applies this to the child and the family. The fact that subjective moral decisions are also made at this point concerning what are proper and acceptable standards of parenting is now open to question (Thorpe 1994). Some children continue to be seen as vulnerable and in need of care, protection and education in order to 'progress' to the status of an adult 'citizen' (Mayall 1996). The third trend is that the child has no voice; no avenue to advance an opinion.

In addition, the image of a vulnerable child is sometimes commodified. Some children's charities, advertizing for funds, use commercialized and powerful images of the 'silent child', with its expressionless face staring into the camera, as an image reminiscent of the bygone Victorian era. Piper (1999) has noted that this image is very powerful; it is is enigmatic, compelling and well marketed. It brings together many compelling images and presents many questions (Kitzinger 1990; Thorpe 1994). Is this child abused? How did it happen? What is the remedy? Such pictures provoke attention and are designed to invoke sympathy and encourage cash donations. The image of the 'abused child' can be manipulated to match the popular, saleable and highly emotive construction of child abuse. Such images stand for the institution and ideal of childhood, free from actual flesh and blood children (Kitzinger 1990). They are dictated by commercialization and can be changed as the market changes without reference to any *real* child. This approach to financing child welfare services would seem to be somewhat anachronistic in societies that claim to have a 'welfare state'. It could be argued that this commercial approach presents a rather simplistic view of the phenomenon of child abuse.

The construction of the 'silent child' in the child protection discourse is one that has been commented upon by a number of authors (e.g. Wattam 1992; Buckley *et al.* 1997; Parton *et al.* 1997). The 'silent child' presents an image of a child abuse victim who is outwardly fearful, withdrawn and neglected. Perhaps, a child may look like that. However, as pointed out by Kitzinger (1990), children who have been abused are rarely passive and often present with anger as well as fear, having steadfastly attempted to avoid the abuse.

There is a tendency to overlook children who do not fit the stereotype of presenting as fearful and disturbed, so they are not recognized as possible 'victims' of abuse (Blagg 1989). It is not uncommon for a child guidance service to receive a referral from a school in respect of a child with aggressive behaviour. Such a referral is generally accompanied by the suggestion that the child needs help to control this behaviour. However, upon further assessment it is revealed that the child has been the victim of child sexual abuse. This underlying problem was not evident to the referring agency as the child had not fitted their stereotype.

Even where a child has been acknowledged as having been abused, their acting-out behaviour is often interpreted pathologically, and consequently they are regarded as a passive victim of abuse. Davies (1995) refers to the child or adult who enters into a 'healing discourse' and then encounters the 'medicalization and psychologization' of sexual abuse. They are regarded as having suffered some deep psychological insult and, therefore, are in need of treatment when in fact their behaviour may be a normal active response to the experienced abuse. Moreover, according to the feminist perspective, the focus on the child as being problematic and maladjusted diverts attention from the socially and politically sanctioned abuse of male power (Davies 1995). This perspective holds that children are rarely passive in these situations, and to adopt a medical model of their behaviour can further victimize them (Kelly 1988).

Another occasion where the child is not 'seen' may occur during the initial referral period. Early reported information can bias the investigation from the outset and the recorded content regarded as fact until proved otherwise. Many workers categorize clients into preconceived classifications from the referral information and their own personal repertoire of experiences (Wattam 1992; Buckley *et al.* 1997). Additionally, assessment of a child may occur through the categorization of their mother and not in terms of the child's current behaviour, which presumably is the subject of the referral (Parton *et al.* 1997). Such categorization could be seen to be a natural way of functioning, especially for newer or more inexperienced practitioners. After all, nature abhors a vacuum and people feel insecure unless they are able to structure their environment and *categorize* (Lawrence 1996). However, it is incumbent on supervisors to be aware of this phenomenon and advise the child protection worker accordingly.

Recent research has also pointed to the 'absent' or 'silent child', where the child's age and gender appear to be the only variables recorded as representations of the child in the notes of child protection practitioners (Kitzinger 1990; Wattam 1992; Davies 1995; Parton *et al.* 1997). The child's perspective is noted to be conspicuous by its absence. Paperwork and proformas have been generated in the bureaucratizaton of child protection work that purport to diminish some of the workload of practitioners, help set criteria and enhance information retrieval (Howe 1992). However, in so doing there is the danger of impersonality and of losing the child as an individual (Skehill *et al.* 1999).

A practitioner may develop a mindset that regards form completion as a prime task, so biasing their assessment accordingly. Bureaucratic procedures designed to control events and impose order may be useful tools, but may also be used to a harmful degree if they are part of a defensive practice that only offers a snapshot of a child, particularly in a residential or daycare setting. Paperwork can be overwhelming to a worker already pressed with a difficult and weighty caseload. As abuse itself rarely lends itself to physical signs and symptoms, brief 'covering' notes made in a child's record may be felt to be the most defensible way forward for the practitioner.

King (1997: 61) has pointed out that certain systems, such as the child protection services, are aware of these underlying paradoxes in their work and will develop strategies to prevent them from rising to the surface. Such a system can generate forms that mean, for some practitioners, that the work will be with the paper and not with the persons concerned. This may be seen as a particular danger for managers who have a primarily administrative role.

Notions of childhood innocence, social anxiety and protectionism

There is much agreement that the child protection discourse continues to promulgate a construction of childhood innocence (Boyden 1990; Kitzinger 1990; Jenks 1996). The major tenets of contemporary rights and welfare thinking are based upon this construction of childhood. That is, the regulation of a child's life should give priority to making childhood carefree, safe, secure and a happy phase of human existence (Boyden 1990). This view has many unintended and negative consequences for children, families and society in the management of such issues such as child sexual abuse. These are described by Kitzinger (1990), who comments on the inherent contradictions within the construction of 'childhood innocence' and outlines three areas that demonstrate why using this concept is problematic:

1   such descriptions may serve as sources of continued arousal for child abusers;
2   it serves to stigmatize a child who may have been abused or who is regarded as too 'knowing' about sexual matters; and
3   such an ideology may be used to deny children access to knowledge and increases their availability to abusers.

In general, such principles create a siege mentality, putting a burden on carers (generally the women), and encourage children to live in fear and maintain adults at arm's length (Smart 1989; Kitzinger 1990; Thorpe 1994; Parton *et al.* 1997). We see therefore that there is a problem inherent in the current construction of childhood that describes children as 'vulnerable'. Feminist perspectives that have stressed the unequal rights of parents over children have highlighted this vulnerability at times of divorce and during access settlements. In these situations, children might be nominally consulted, but decisions about their care are made by others 'in their best interests' (Smart and Sevenhuijsen 1989). The child's voice, even if heard, is rarely given prominence.

The contemporary vision of childhood innocence and vulnerability that renders children in need of protection is maintained by the media, politicians, paediatrics and psychology (Parton 1985, 1991; Boydon 1990;

Kitzinger 1990; Howitt 1992; Jenks 1996; Leonard 1997). As society holds to this view of childhood innocence there exists the moral opinion that those who violate such sanctity are monsters and perverts. Public outcry directed against paedophilia is common and gives it 'banner' headlines. Children in this sense are the symbols of good and their violators the symbols of evil (King 1997). As Kitzinger (1990: 177–8) has pointed out, 'Assault and exploitation are risks inherent to "childhood" as it is currently lived'.

Discussion in regard to what has provoked this contemporary interest in childhood and its violation stems from the collective anxiety of society (King 1999). The media highlighting of grievously serious individual cases taps into a collective sense of moral indignation. With no external enemy upon whom to release this anxiety, people find other targets for its expression. King refers to public anxieties over safe meat, war and children who still remain 'at risk' of abuse. He maintains that reassurances from governments have the paradoxical effect of sounding feeble and consequently generate even more anxiety.

Society and its information technology is now said to have commodified knowledge *and* morality (King 1999). In contemporary society, previously formed points of attachment for individuals with a collective life such as class, work groups and local community have greatly diminished (Leonard 1997). In this world view, childhood is said to remain as a symbol of a lost ideal of primary human relationships. There is nostalgia for the pleasure and security of a life past, now invested in the child. Similarly, Jenks (1996) links the contemporary heightened attention to those who would violate children to society's collective pain from the loss of its own identity. He goes on to say that alterations in the family have seen a breakdown in marriage and an intensification of relationality in respect of children. Again, a collective anxiety seems to permeate a society that is intolerant of risk and uncertainty. This state of being is the projection of the individual's own need for comfort that stems from an alienation from points of attachment to a collective life (Hage and Powers 1992). In such a society, children are the embodiment of the last vestige of the social bond. Child sexual abuse *then* becomes a crime against 'childhood' itself (Kitzinger 1990). However, this idealized childhood is often far from the real life experience of children in contemporary society.

The foregoing account of idealized and sometimes fantasized notions of childhood, with its attendant notions of vulnerability, is open to challenge. In the first place, recent document analysis has indicated that there are degrees of abuse on a continuum from mild to grievous. Second, although extreme cases of abuse are in the minority, they do occupy a disproportionate amount of press and political time (Wattam 1992; Cooper 1993; Thorpe 1994). Third, the problem is not new, nor is it uncommon.

Fourth, projections of child abuse have often been abstracted and applied without reference to the real lives of the child or the family involved. The children who are then seen in these ideal and abstract terms may be further drawn away from the day-to-day experiences of their lives with their parents, their housing, their neighbourhoods, their class, their culture and their ethnicity.

A further challenge to the popular perception of childhood perpetuated in the media is the notion that child abuse can be predicted and controlled. Adopting a positivist approach, rational systems of operation are then designed to control the risks of abuse in society using the 'scientific approach'. Sanctions against those held to be responsible are applied if things go wrong. When abuse occurs, pathology is individuated and blame is the logical outcome for 'failure' or exceptions to the norms. The contemporary child protection industry has been organized around such pseudo-scientific and rational conceptions of risks, their assessment and their predictive outcomes. This view can be challenged in the light of recent research by Kitzinger (1990), Wattam (1992), Thorpe (1994) and Parton *et al.* (1997). A refocusing of the construction of childhood and matters of child welfare is now occurring. The aforementioned authors refer to a more subjectivist approach and advocate a retreat from scientific notions of risk calculation in assessment, to more individual notions of uncertainty that occur in situated moral judgements (Parton 1998).

The globalization of 'ideal' childrearing practices in isolation from the real world of children and their parents has been achieved through a somewhat narrow interpretation of 'the rights of the child' (Thorpe 1994). Realizing the ideal of human rights implementation without seeing the child *in situ* is a challenge for contemporary child welfare. Emphasis on the pursuit of children's rights, representing them in the media, legislation and governmental directives via terms such as 'abused', 'maltreatment' and 'child protection' all lead to an abstract conception of children, sanitized from reality (Thorpe 1994). The decontextualizing of children in this way ignores a host of other social, economic and political factors that need to be acknowledged when describing the 'real child'.

Child protection discourses that follow the pursuit of such reified goals have, in the words of Thorpe (1994: 199), 'succeeded in changing the role of child welfare agencies from predominantly one of service provision, to one of policing and "normalizing"'. The challenge for child welfare is to promote the well-being of children by encouraging and supporting their parents, rather than through a type of policing that appears to act on behalf of children but, in effect, may present a barrier within the family. There is a need to clarify some issues of children's rights and whether we can clearly say in today's society if there is any absolute notion of rights or wrongs for children.

Children's rights

Prior to the late nineteenth century, the state seldom intervened in the life of the family (Kaul 1983; Campbell 1988; Fox Harding 1991a, 1991b). Legislative intervention was only achieved at that time when the social costs of wasted human resources were recognized and family violence threatened to spill over into the public arena. May (1978) states further that in the 1870s there was a marked growing public awareness of the extent of child abuse which culminated in the foundation of the NSPCC and the first salient legislation, The Prevention of Cruelty to Children Act 1889. Similar voluntary societies were subsequently organized in Australia. Western Australia's first Children's Act was promulgated in 1908 and the state Children's Department was established in the same year.

In England, the establishment of the welfare state in the 1950s was a milestone in social services generally, and coincided with the establishment of childcare services (Parton 1991). The social intervention of the state into family life that had been inaugurated and held as a model for society at the time, later began to be questioned as the political climate changed in the 1970s and the 1980s. After a series of child deaths during these decades, the public inquiries put the responsibility of failing to protect children firmly on the social services of the day. Similarly, the Cleveland Report was notable for its criticism of the intervention of social services into family matters (Campbell 1988). More recently, in England the government Green Paper *Every Child Matters* (DfES 2003) has initiated pilot programmes as a first step to improve services for children by combining social services with education and health.

It was not until 1959 that the international community at the United Nations General Assembly issued its first *Declaration of the Rights of the Child*. Cooper (1993) commends this document as it acknowledges that the state, as well as individual carers, has a responsibility for children. Further to this, the emphasis here was on goals rather than on working definitions – a recognition that different societies have different priorities about child abuse.

It was in the 1980s that children's rights came of age, when they were raised in the context of concern about moral and political status as well as social and welfare needs. Most of the discussions prior to the 1980s concerning children's rights had been theoretical and concerned with general considerations. In so doing, they had often overlooked practical suggestions for change. Since that time, more practical policy and institutional reforms have been suggested, such as *ombudswork* for children. Franklyn (1995b: 15) refers to the appointment of such an officer in Leicestershire in 1988, as an example of the actual fulfilment of one of these suggestions.

As of 2003, the post of national Children's Rights Commissioner is now established in Wales and Northern Ireland, with plans in England and Scotland to follow suit. Despite the interest in the rights of children, for the most part governments have shown little concern for introducing legislation to empower and protect these rights. It is encouraging to note that the British Labour Party's proposal in 1992 for the appointment of a Minister for Children has now become a reality. However, the British government has yet to incorporate the United Nations *Declaration on the Rights of the Child* into law along with the proposed changes as outlined in Every Child Matters (DfES 2003). A parliamentary group for primary care and public health are currently putting pressure on the government to do so.

Although the *Declaration on the Rights of the Child* is regarded as a significant development in promoting the rights of children, to date not all governments have ratified it, and nor have they abided by its proposals. Some countries have displayed a reluctance to meet its commitments. There is even one example on record of a breach of the *Declaration* in Western Australia, where indeterminate sentencing of juvenile offenders has been introduced (Rayner 1995).

The *Declaration* was signed by the General Assembly on 20 November 1989. This was seen to be a considerably strengthened document from the original proposal introduced in 1959. Before the end of the 1990s, individual nation signatories were asked to report to the United Nations on their progress in implementing the *Declaration*. After consideration among all of its six states and two territories, Australia ratified the document in December 1990 (Rayner 1995). The *Declaration* was ratified by the UK in December 1991 (Jones and Bilton 1994). While it has been said that the *Declaration* has been a significant development intended to promote and protect children's rights, there has been a reluctance in some countries to meet its commitments (Franklyn 1995b). Some reasons for this have to do with a lack of cross-cultural agreement regarding definitions about childhood in respect of age, cultural constructs, state allocation of resources and individual state legislation. The highly multicultural society of Australia is a particular example of these difficulties. The increasing cultural diversity in the UK is now equally feeling the pressure of forging a sensitive cultural response to the differing mores of diverse ethnic groups. The task of taking into account cultural differences in attitudes to children's rights and enforcing the child's statutory right to protection from harm has been seen by many as a limitation to parental freedom.

Statements about children's rights frequently take two forms. The first concerns what is due to a child from the significant people in whose care they are placed – usually the parents, the state and its agencies. The second is concerned with rights that invest power and authority in the child to exercise choices and decisions. As pointed out by Jones and Bilton (1994), it appears to be symptomatic of children's dependent status that their rights are most commonly expressed in terms of what is due to them from others. The respecting of rights turns out to be not so much one of assertion and compliance as one of negotiation and compromize. There appears to be a paradox here. On the one hand, it is argued that children should have more autonomy, and on the other hand, it is the adults who are placed in the position of protecting children to ensure their rights. So in effect children remain relatively disempowered.

The distinction between two types of children's rights suggested by Franklyn (1995b) may go some way to resolving this paradox. There are the rights to *provision* and *protection* on the one hand, and the right to *participation* on the other. The former have been termed 'passive' and the later termed 'active'. This is similar to the distinction made by Cunningham (1991) between rights that are to do with guaranteeing levels of treatment by adults, as in healthcare and education, which contrast with rights of self-determination such as the right to work, vote and travel. In this sense, childhood has a restricted citizenship. The democratic and participating child may be a limited concept and is probably contingent on the age and competency of the child. While some children may be capable of self-determination at some stage, children are not a homogeneous group and most remain dependent on adults and are subject to the current legislation of the day that emphasizes parental responsibilities. The *Declaration* has not resolved the dilemma, as it seems to confuse the child's need for protection with emphasis on autonomous participation (Buckingham 2000). Anomalies exist throughout a child's life world. One example would be the 16-year-old who is expected to pay taxes if gainfully employed, but is not allowed to vote.

In the UK, the 1948 Children Act was an attempt to end the paternalism of 'rescuing' children from their families. Efforts were made to keep children and families together and local authorities had a duty to rehabilitate children with their families of natural origin wherever possible (Reder *et al.* 1993). Children's departments were established to administer existing services to families, but with an emphasis on gaining voluntary cooperation and mutual agreement with parents, in the best interests of the child. This was a different philosophy from that which had previously existed. However, despite this optimism, legislation continued to view children in terms of welfare paternalism and professionals were able to intervene in the family without having to take into account the views or wishes of parents (Lyon and Parton 1995). Ambiguity about the rights of children and parents prevailed.

The Children Act 1989 in England and Wales was a legislative milestone in the history of childcare and children's rights, reinforcing the promotion of the welfare of children in the family. In addition it sought a governmental balance to include the supremacy of children's rights while promoting the need to work in partnership with parents and also maintaining the protective role of the state. But even this document presents dilemmas concerning the rights of children, parents and the state to involve itself in the protection of children. Lyon and Parton (1995) report that while the Children Act 1989 does appear to take the rights of children seriously and provides new opportunities for advancing these rights, it does so in a qualified manner. For example, there are features of the Act that emphasize the duty of professionals to work in partnership with parents and act in defence of the natural family, but at the same time they are expected to focus on the rights of the child and to give the child a voice.

Fox Harding (1991a, 1991b) identified four main strands of thinking in the Children Act 1989, as listed below.

1   *Laissez-faire and patriarchy*: a minimalist intervention stance adopted by the state in family affairs. This approach does not challenge the *status quo* and so implicitly upholds a patriarchal system.
2   *State paternalism and child protection*: a stance that allows for greater state intervention to uphold the welfare of the child as a paramount goal and lessen the rights of parents.
3   *Defence of the birth family and parents' rights*: where the state role is to be positively supportive of both parents and children and the parent-child bond.
4   *Children's rights and child liberation*: the focus is upon the empowerment of children with their right to have a say in decisions affecting their own lives. The control of children either through state or adults is called into question.

In this analysis of the Act, the competing tensions in the legislation relate primarily to two issues (Morrison 1996). The first is that while increasing the state's right to intervene in family life there is also the principle of judicial non-intervention. Second, there is the emphasis on parents' rights and the importance of working in partnership with parents with the counterbalance of upholding children's rights.

Two of the most notable aims of the Children Act 1989 were to reinforce the rights of parents and children to be free of state intervention and to limit the need for the state to intervene in family life. Unfortunately, the potential of these aims has not been fully grasped, let alone achieved. Failure to adequately resource the Act was a major omission. Law takes precedence on matters of child abuse and the focus of child protection assessments is now on investigation, the collection of evidential statements and the forensic substantiation of abuse. This entails a diminished therapeutic role for the child protection practitioner.

A strong feature of the Children Act 1989 in England and Wales and the Child Welfare Act 1989 in Western Australia is that the child's welfare rights are given precedence over parental rights, wherever there may be a conflict. In these countries, parents, or those who have this responsibility, are entitled to autonomy and privacy. Clear delineation is made in the Acts regarding the conditions that would warrant state intervention, bearing in mind the possible loss of parental rights (Archard 1993). In Western Australia, the state can choose to grant an immediate 48-hour legal power of *in loco parentis* to intervene on behalf of the safety and welfare of a child. The matter then will need to proceed to a court for a furtherance of the decree. Decisions will then follow through appointed state representatives who determine what is in the best interests of the child: if they are to be returned home or if alternative arrangements need to be made. As this is a socio-legal decision, the child's circumstances are more often than not seen in terms of substantiated evidential harms or risk of future harms. The child, depending upon age and developmental standard, may be asked for an opinion but, as in cases of separation, divorce and access arrangements it is generally the concerned adults who are the decision-makers. The reason for this is that the child's competency is often open to question. As developmental psychology has pointed out, the child is still progressing toward the adult ideal of rationality (Piaget 1974). The child as victim and in need of rescue remains a dominant construction in the child protection discourse of most current welfare practices.

It can be seen that the Children Act 1989 set out to promote childcare, children's welfare, children's rights and the rights of parents from a number of different perspectives. Jeffries *et al.* (1997: 2) refer to Fox Harding's view that 'the Children Act has placed more emphasis on the paternalistic and pro-birth family perspectives'. The Act was a laudable attempt to balance the rights of children, their parents and the responsibilities of the state. However, it can be appreciated that there are a number of ambiguities to be resolved in practice.

For some interested parties, the formalization of children's rights is perceived as a threat to their own rights. Traditionally, the educational system view of children is that they have to be controlled and organized and so they are left relatively disempowered. The law gives pupils no statutory right to be heard in educational decision-making. A further example of interested parties being threatened by the formalization of children's rights is outlined by Smart (1989) with regard to custody arrangements following a divorce, where some have argued for greater legal control of children outside marriage.

Cooper (1993) asserts that the preoccupation with children's rights has often created a social unease and an antagonistic situation. The advocacy of human rights from a theoretical high ground may be inadequate and arguably counterproductive, unless the focus of attention is directed away from the adversarial (Rayner 1995). In Australia, before the ratification of the *Convention on the Rights of the Child* in 1991, there were controversial issues about its meaning, such as the loss of parental authority to the state and of Australian sovereignty to the international community as represented by the United Nations.

There are times when rights are enforced in such a manner that they appear to deliberately restrict the freedom of children, as when a child's right to education is enforced by a duty to receive it, or when there is an imposition of curfews (Buckingham 2000). Moreover, the balancing of public and parental obligations with children's freedom changes as children develop. The interplay between these factors of state obligation and the freedom of the child is of growing interest in such fields as education, health and child guidance work. One example of this is in regard to custody arrangements following divorce. Other examples are when some children refuse to attend school or reject medical help.

As can be seen, the establishment and management of a service for the sexually abused child should be organized within the broader context of human rights. Unfortunately, human rights tend often to be of low priority in economic planning. The implementation of such rights is inconvenient and costly, and sometimes governments try to avoid it (Rayner 1995). Whatever the fluctuations of governmental economy, we cannot afford to lose sight of fundamental human rights in general, or of children's rights in particular.

Summary

This chapter has reviewed the social constructions of childhood. It is apparent that childhood, as an identifiable construct, was absent in early sociological theory. There had been an apparent blindness with regard to childhood as a distinct category. It had been subsumed within the institutions of the family and education. Parallels with the contemporary sociological interest in the body are evident.

As society moved from a mainly agrarian-based economy to an industrialized one, the role of children changed and they began to be perceived as a separate group. Once childhood was recognized as a separate category, the place of children in society was debated. As a visible group, it became acknowledged that children needed protection from exploitation and they were also deemed to be in need of societal regulation. In particular, this regulation was thought necessary to protect society from those children showing delinquent behaviour. Laws were introduced to protect children from exploitation in the workplace and compulsory schooling was enforced.

By the end of the nineteenth century, although society was making provisions for children as a group, sociology had still not recognized childhood as a separate category outside the family and education, but had conceded the study of childhood to psychology. Psychology, at this time, had adopted the positivistic approach established in the physical sciences. Thus, childhood was studied, researched and ordered by establishing norms of growth and stages in children's development. Moreover, children were viewed as if they were mostly passive objects developing through stages and without reference to the social context of their development.

Later recognition by psychology and sociology of the social context of child development has reinforced childhood as a distinct category of study. Once this was recognized, it became possible to study the constructions of childhood over significant periods of time. This study revealed the impact of economic, social and cultural influences. The acknowledgement of childhood as a social construction is now well established in contemporary literature, and childhood has emerged as a separate area of study for sociology.

In the next chapter the development of professional regulation of child abuse and child sexual abuse will be discussed with special reference to the contemporary child protection discourse.

3　The child protection discourse

Introduction

This chapter begins with an overview of the periodization of professional regulation of child abuse and the development of the contemporary child protection discourse. Particular attention is paid to the original child health and welfare issues of the past century. The history of the concept of child abuse management is traced and criticisms of the orthodox scientific-medical discourse of child abuse are presented. These issues are discussed in relation to the increasingly legalistic regulation of child protection practice and the backlash against this method of regulation.

The main challenges that surround the child protection discourse in contemporary practice are outlined. The effectiveness of services for children and families working within the strictly positivist framework is questioned. The use of some mandated interventions, involving a positivist framework, has been reported to cause additional distress to abuse victims. This is known as 'secondary victimization', and is discussed in this chapter. Further challenges to child protection practice relate to working in partnership with parents. These are often created by the dilemma of official intervention in family life and, at the same time, the need to establish a therapeutic relationship with families.

The traditional use of an ill-defined at risk category of possible abuse is presented as a further challenge to practice. The chapter concludes with a discussion of the failure of current systems of child protection to recognize 'chronic child abuse'. This is of particular importance as the opportunity to address the implications of poverty for families is often unacknowledged.

Periodization of the professional regulation of child abuse and child sexual abuse

Most discussions of the history of modern child protection systems freely acknowledge the origins of those systems in the nineteenth-century voluntary sector (Howitt 1992; Piper 1999). There was a gradual profession-alization of child protection, stimulated by concern shown by the clergy, educationalists and the medical profession. Scientific advances in technology allowed for a more thorough examination of childhood illness and mortality, and this revealed such things as venereal diseases among children, infant mortality due to lack of adequate nutrition, physical maltreatment and cruelty to children by the owners of factories. As a result of these events, child abuse became an established social phenomenon in the early twentieth century.

Despite this recognition of child abuse as a social problem, the social work literature of the 1900s up to the 1950s presented child abuse as a general phenomenon and certainly not one warranting intervention by community agents: 'So silent is this period on abuse that authors are able to write about the "rediscovery of child abuse" in the latter part of the twentieth century' (Howitt 1992: 18). Following this period of quiescence up to the end of the 1950s, there was a rapid growth in the public child welfare system, first in the USA, with the UK and Australia following soon after (Boss 1980; Kadushin and Martin 1988; Cooper 1993). The child welfare systems of this period were primarily set up to respond to child neglect and abuse.

As discussed in the previous chapter, specific childcare and child welfare issues became prominent in the 1960s with the scientific-medical identification of abuse (Kempe *et al.* 1962) and the advocacy of children's rights. Behind these welfare systems was an optimistic unitary belief in progress and a positivistic belief in the value of the medical-scientific approach as a basis for the focus of the emerging professionals, such as social workers, psychologists and paediatricians (O'Hagan 1989; Parton *et al.* 1997). The emphasis in this general welfare approach was on therapeutic intervention, nurturing model and psychological theories. The law was seen only as a basis for mandated intervention: 'The overall rationale of welfarism was to make the liberal market society and the family more productive, stable and harmonious; and the role of the government, while more complex and expansive, would be positive and beneficent' (Parton 1998: 12). The model of child abuse at this time was seen in terms of the medical-scientific approach, also known as the public health model (Parton 1985; Lindsay 1994). Child abuse was assumed to be an illness that required clinical investigation for its identification and treatment. The condition was often thought to be hidden, especially by parents, and needed a team of specialists to uncover the problem.

During the late 1960s and early 1970s, a belief in the hidden nature of the problem gave support to professionals' actions on behalf of a child deemed to be at 'risk'. Concerns became legitimate if clinical suspicion was aroused. While the focus was on the verification of abuse through observable signs, it was 'silently' acknowledged among some hospital medical staff that sometimes there were suspicions of abuse without there being any substantiating evidence.

It would not have been uncommon in these instances for the physician in a children's hospital to write, 'BBS?' in a child's medical notes prior to 1980, meaning 'Query: Battered Baby Syndrome' (Griffiths and Moynihan 1963). The letters were used to indicate that the physician had queried whether abuse *might* be occurring. Similarly, other symbols might be employed in a children's hospital as signs to alert other staff that there were suspicions about a particular episode. For example, a system of placing a red triangle on a child's medical notes might be used to indicate that either they had been abused in the past or that medical staff had grounds for thinking that the child might be 'at risk of abuse'. However, this same red triangle was also placed on the medical notes of other children if they had 'special' medical conditions that required extra care and attention. Either way, the red triangle was meant to stand for a high-risk patient. This silent language system was gradually replaced by protocols for discussion of such issues that significantly included the parents, and the red triangles gradually disappeared in the 1980s. In addition, the terms 'battered child syndrome' (Kempe *et al.* 1962) and 'battered baby syndrome' (Griffiths and Moynihan 1963) were gradually replaced in the 1970s with the less medicalised term 'non-accidental injury' (NAI).

In regard to child sexual abuse, there had been social and legal recognition of the phenomenon for a century or more, but it was only from the 1970s that it received societal and professional prominence. Howitt (1992) provides us with a description of society's recognition of this evolving phenomenon in the recent past when he quotes the incest statistics for England and Wales from 1950 through to 1989.

There was little publicity and no common public pressure about known cases of incest prior to the 1970s and no widespread recognition of the problem of child sexual abuse, even as a topic of enquiry among professionals until the early 1980s (Campbell 1988; DHSS 1988; Lawrence 1990). In England, it is said that the 'new consciousness' dates from 1983, when a television documentary exposed the harassment of a rape victim (Campbell 1988). Thereafter, several police forces conceived the idea of recruiting women doctors to examine the victims of sexual abuse. This soon became a service for children. At the same time in Western Australia, rape crisis centres that had been established for adults were asked to cater for children. A separate sexual abuse clinic for children in Western Australia was established in 1982 at the children's hospital in that state.

According to Finklehor (1982), prior to 1970 child sexual abuse had only been recognized by a segment of the population, such as the second generation feminist movement and other social reformers, who at that time had little credibility in the eyes of many male-dominated professions and policy-makers. Those who expressed their concern that children were being sexually abused because of the liberalization of sexual mores were seen as moralists and alarmists. They were said to have used this issue as a way of campaigning against other kinds of progressive reform that most social welfare professionals supported – for example, sex education, humane treatment of sex offenders and censorship. Finklehor comments that the error of this original group was to identify the greatest danger to children as coming from strangers – depraved people, outside the family – and not from *inside* where more serious threats were then being documented.

The 1970s and 1980s saw a profound development in community awareness concerning the issues of child abuse in general and child sexual abuse in particular. Child sexual abuse, which had been reported rarely until the 1970s, began to be more generally recognized as one of the major social problems of the time. The burgeoning number of cases, debates within multidisciplinary teams about their management, and financial cutbacks all contributed to a crisis of confidence undercutting the optimism that had been evident prior to the mid-1970s (Morrison 1996; Parton *et al.* 1997). Economic downturns and growing social deprivation, the rise in violence and social changes to the family and society created serious problems for the continuance of the welfare ambitions pre-1960.

Critiques of the service delivery appeared from every political direction. In the mid-1970s the Conservative government in England sought to introduce new, more conservative, service provisions and change to the organization of services (Parton 1998). This was also supported by the criticisms from the opposing political front that were represented by advocates from the women's movement, the children's rights movement and the 'civil liberty' groups of parents, all of whom emphasized individual rights. Thus, the growth of the 'civil liberties' critique, which concentrated on the apparent extent and nature of intervention into people's lives that was allowed, unchallenged, in the name of welfare' 'had gathered momentum from the late 1960s' (Parton *et al.* 1997: 27). Legalism had entered the childcare and welfare arena in response to the inability of the socio-medical model alone to be an accurate indicator or predicator with regard to the occurrence of child abuse.

There were also serious questions emanating 'from within social work itself [concerning] the apparent poor and ... deteriorating quality of child care practice in the [then] newly created social service departments' (Parton 1991: 195).' The combination of these events, the recommendations for change and the backlash of opinions converged with a number of government inquiries to expose the shortfalls in the child welfare system of the 1980s. These political, legal and social circumstances formed the prelude to what Parton (1998: 13) refers to as the 'advanced liberal' society and the development of the child protection system.

The development of the child protection discourse

The contemporary discourse of child protection began in the aftermath of the child abuse inquiries in England and eventually had an impact world-wide (Buckley *et al.* 1997; Parton 1998). There had been an explosion of these public inquiries in England, most of which concerned cases of fatal child abuse in the 1960s and 1970s (Reder *et al.* 1993). Parton (1998) has referred to the inquiries as providing avenues for the venting of criticisms of policy and practice in child welfare and also in regard to the judging of the competencies of social workers themselves. Child abuse and plans for the state to intervene in family life in protecting children from harm were now subjects of open public and political debate.

These inquiry reports drew the public's attention to management errors that were considered to be a result of social workers failing to intervene and prevent cases of child abuse. This led to what has been referred to as a 'moral panic' (Parton 1985; Cooper 1993; King 1997). The phenomenon of a moral panic is the expression or outpouring of intense social anxiety about an identified social problem by the public (sometimes thought of as being the 'silent majority') and accompanied by the demand that something be done to resolve the situation. In addition, moral panics are said to develop during periods of rapid social change, are usually media-led and are vocal in their condemnation of persons who are perceived as a threat to social values and structures (Hall *et al.* 1978; Parton 1985; Best 1989; Robin 1991; Cooper 1993). Cooper (1993) has added that a moral panic demonstrates a breakdown in general consensus, a need to lay blame and the search for culprits or scapegoats. The displacement of anger in the aftermath of the child abuse inquiries fell on the social work profession, who were considered to be in need of regulation through extended governmental procedures and guidelines.

The implication of 'blaming the social worker' seemed to be that all cases of child abuse could be eradicated if only the professionals involved were doing their work properly. It has been suggested by Parton (1985) that the venting of this moral outrage and the criticism of the individuals involved diverted attention from the sociological factors associated with the causes of abuse. It was also suggested that the vilification of social workers appeased the public need for something to be done about the problem.

The inquiry reports refined and recommended new policy and procedure guidelines. The new policy advocated in these reports reminded social workers of their legal mandate to intervene on behalf of abused children. Area child protection committees, case conferences and registers of child abuse cases were established to enhance interagency work and individual case management. However, there was little complementary focus on treatment and prevention. With each successive inquiry report there were accumulating policy guidelines that were referred to by Howe (1992) as the 'bureaucratisation of social work'.

As new forms of abuse and abusive families were recognized, governmental directives helped to identify 'dangerous' families where child abuse was likely to occur (Parton 1991). The phenomenon of 'diagnostic inflation', as identified by Dingwall (1989) was now in evidence, with a successive growth in not only the types of abuse but also in the number of governmental checklists produced in an attempt to help identify and prevent the problem from occurring.

The legal model

New procedures and guidelines were also provided for social workers to identify and calculate the degree of risk of abuse in assessments of children and families. The inquiries were criticized for having studied social work through a judicial lens that focused on the worst case scenarios of child abuse (Parton 1991; Reder, *et al.* 1993). It has also been argued that the inquiries resulted in undue emphasis being placed on the creation of policy that exerted legal authority over social workers. Decisions in regard to child protection cases were to be made only after full legal consideration in a multidisciplinary case conference (DoH 1991b; Parton *et al.* 1997). The social workers' role now appeared to shift from a therapeutic relationship with clients to that of a 'soft' police role. The emphasis was now mainly on investigation to collect forensic evidence for presentation to courts. The focus on the signs of child abuse had begun to shift away from the socio-medical model alone to include the legal framework.

Social workers now appeared to be moving towards what has been described as a 'no win situation'. On the one hand, they were criticized in the numerous child abuse inquiries for doing too little too late (Morrison 1996: 128). Thereafter, they were situated in the legal discourse of the state's role in protecting children and were encouraged to be more proactive in the battle against child abuse. The mid-1980s then brought to the public's attention the events of the management of child sexual abuse in Cleveland, England. In the ensuing *Cleveland Report* (Butler-Sloss 1988), social workers were accused of doing too much too soon (Morrison 1996).

In England, the second half of the 1980s saw a distinct period of change in the law and in childcare practice that helped shape the 'child protection industry', as it is sometimes called (Adler 1996). The events that surrounded the Cleveland child sexual abuse scandals and the ensuing aftermath in the latter half of the 1980s are reported by Parton *et al.* (1997) to have been the watershed that determined the contemporary nature of child protection.

The events in Cleveland centred on children who were being diagnosed as sexually abused being removed from their homes by social workers and taken to places of safety. It was soon revealed that the medical diagnoses the children had been given could not stand in court as proof of sexual abuse. The children's statements had been taken in the context of a pre-judged situation and the parents had had no right of reply (Wattam 1992). The initial 'disclosure of abuse' made by children in these circumstances was discredited in a legal context because of the biased nature of the interview (Parton *et al.* 1997). In addition, the large numbers of children involved contributed to public mayhem as well as putting undue strain on child protection services. Poor interdisciplinary communication and lack of trust between the professionals added to scepticism about the truth of the 'disclosures' and contributed to a breakdown in interagency functioning.

An official inquiry into these events was published in the Cleveland Report (Butler-Sloss 1988). This was the first official report to investigate the management of the phenomenon of child sexual abuse, and underscored the need for a change in the law and also for improvements to be made in interagency coordination and collaboration. The report began a distinct change in emphasis away from a medical-scientific model in the identification of child abuse towards a more legalistic and evidential framework. This new approach, the seeds of which had been sown in previous inquiry reports, now continued with a pseudo-scientific approach, but changed the emphasis of the work, placing central importance on joint working between the police and the social services in the investigation of child sexual abuse.

The newly recommended legal framework, within which social work practitioners were to operate, brought with it a new construction and interpretation of investigation and the need for the gathering of evidence (Wattam 1992). This change in emphasis also occurred in Australia, where the Cleveland Report also had an impact. The term 'child protection discourse' had now come into being and superseded the term 'child abuse management'. The emphasis changed from identifying clinical signs of abuse to identifying *signs of risk*. Children could now only be protected on the basis of clear, legally formulated evidence. In both England and Australia, this meant that social workers were expected to work more closely with the police and the legal departments of their services. In England, the Department of Health (DoH 1995) recommended procedures for the video-taping of children's testimony for use as evidence in the courtroom. The result was a new investigative role for social workers with a concentration on collecting forensic evidence.

In Australia too, the 'language' of the child protection discourse was becoming common currency among child protection workers. This language was in part the result of international exchange through the media, professional journal articles, national and international conferences and an array of exchange visits of professional staff between England and Australia. There was a gradual change in the language employed in Australia. For example, many of the interdisciplinary teams who had been referred to as 'child abuse teams' were now changing their title to 'child protection teams'.

In the wake of the Cleveland affair, various media reports drew the community's attention to the fact that the child protection system that had been set up to tackle child abuse appeared to have as many negative consequences for children and their families as it did positive ones. Throughout the 1980s, the child protection movement had generated considerable public attention by quoting large numbers of children who had been sexually abused. This alarmed common sensibilities and persuaded the public that something needed to be done. Statistics, which were said to have reached epidemic proportions, helped to generate a moral panic, as referred to earlier, about child sexual abuse and also about the management of the problem. Following Cleveland, social workers and paediatricians were vilified and became the focus of general public anger. The backlash of parents and the public was against the professionals who were seen to have acted prematurely and without due consideration for the rights of parents and families (Parton 1998).

Previously, once the outpouring of the public's anger abated, the multiple problems that caused the hostility would recede from social awareness and remain dormant until another child abuse tragedy was brought to the fore in the media (Reder *et al.* 1993). This time there were ongoing campaigns for the rights of parents and families to be recognized and included in child protection practice decisions. In addition, policy-makers realized that inquiry reports kept identifying the same problems over and over again. Apparently, there had been no successful resolution of these problems (Buckley *et al.* 1997) and past adjustments and additions to the child protection system did not prevent tragedies from continuing to happen. Statistics on child abuse remained high.

These problems, sharply defined by the child sexual abuse controversies in the Cleveland affair, now demanded political intervention. In response, the British government made a large investment into a series of research projects that focused on various unresolved issues of child protection. The results of these investigations were combined in the document, *Child Protection: Messages from Research* (DoH 1995), in which the functioning of the child protection system was investigated and criticized. The scope of the underlying complexities and difficulties received nominal attention, and many of the dilemmas it discussed remained unresolved. In particular, child abuse definitional issues, working in partnership with parents, children's rights and the functioning of interagency coordination and cooperation remained problematic. The report suggested that through careful and further attention, these problems would be resolved. However, it ignored the wider social and economic contexts within which the problems occurred and which clearly were associated with the phenomenon of child abuse.

The scope and the depth of the problem of child sexual abuse had by now achieved political notoriety. In the aftermath of the commissioning of the above research, and following the Cleveland affair, there was a review of social work training in England and Wales and calls for the law to be changed, culminating in the Children Act 1989. Many of the unresolved issues referred to above were also raised in this legislation, particularly those concerning state intervention into family life, rights of children, rights of parents and children in need.

The Children Act 1989 was a milestone in the history of the child protection discourse. Among its many recommendations was an emphasis on parental and children's rights and the necessity of consulting with parents at every stage of an investigation. There was encouragement in the Act to work in partnership with parents. At the same time, the legal framework was regarded as crucial in determining a 'child at risk'. Moreover, for the first time, the Act gave powers for state intervention on the basis of a *prediction* of behaviour. This apparent contradiction is pursued further by Fox Harding (1991a, 1991b), who has made an authoritative criticism of the Act and illustrates that the four main value strands have potentially conflicting interpretations.

There were other major legislative documents that helped shape child protection practices following the Cleveland Report and the Children Act 1989. Notable among these were *Working Together (under the Children Act) 1989* (DoH 1991b), the Criminal Justice Act 1992, the Memorandum of Good Practice and *Working Together to Safeguard Children* (DoH 1999). In these documents, the roles of the police, the legal profession and social services was further developed. These documents placed an emphasis on the following aspects of the child protection investigation process. First, the importance of working in partnership with parents and a stress on interagency and interdisciplinary working in joint investigations was made clear. Second, the criminalization of certain behaviours was to be substantiated with forensic evidence and of pre-recorded video evidence for children's statements was made admissible. Finally, advice on obtaining video evidence from children in order to attain a conviction was introduced. Assessments of risk were no longer left to health and social welfare experts alone, and the accountability for making them was ultimately lodged with the courts (Parton 1998). Although in theory these documents were designed to advance the welfare of children, doubts have been cast as to their value in practice. For example, research findings have indicated that the intense concentration on legalistic and forensic evidence has had a tendency to neglect the wider needs of children and their families (Buckley *et al.* 1997). As the professionals were presented with these approaches and the inherent dilemmas they posed for practice, there was a simultaneous upsurge of disquiet from the public sector. Social workers could still be criticized for failing to intervene soon enough and there was a growing backlash against the child protection discourse throughout the 1990s.

The backlash against child protection

In the 1990s, child protection practice became the subject of a backlash from certain quarters of the population, as described by Myers (1994). Some critics have said that the coalitions formed by multiagency cooperation now assumed postures not only of assistance, but also of potential abuse (Blagg and Stubbs 1988; Evans and Miller 1992; O'Hagan and Dillenburger 1995). Some believed that so powerful were certain organizational coalitions that they posed threats, not only to the children and families they had hoped to help, but also to less powerful agencies who were nonetheless highly involved with families (Evans and Miller 1992; Myers 1994). One of the dangers inherent in the power of such coalitions is that they may seek 'one best answer' and then impose this on an entire population (Parton 1985; Blagg and Stubbs 1988; Thorpe 1994; Ife 1997). Once such coalitions set the standards they are often regarded as the 'experts' and others may defer to them. This perspective was noted by Leonard (1997), who commented that Marxist critics of the social democratic welfare state, in general, would point to the domination of state apparatus and to the inadequacy and inequity of services.

Myers (1994) reminds us that child protection efforts have always been criticized and believes that this is inevitable as intervention in the family usually offends. Myers goes on to say that he considers that intervention is inherently coercive and confrontational. Contemporary welfare practice has acknowledged these criticisms and has identified the need to reconstruct welfare in new directions with a commitment to the development of human health and well-being in general. In the face of past criticism and current reconstruction, there has never been a better time for arguments which are solidly based on research and require planning and quality assurance of the highest order. The situation requires credible research upon which counter arguments can be built and proposals developed for the correction of problem areas, and only in this way will new challenges be appropriately met (Pizzini 1994).

Challenges to child protection practice

As has been noted, child protection interventions in regard to child abuse in general in the 1980s drew increasing public attention and critical media interest. However, the scope and depth of the problem of child *sexual* abuse, in particular, achieved political notoriety and brought to the fore social and legal questions about the rights of children and their families. The moral panic and public pressure on child protection practitioners at the time of the Cleveland affair and the resulting shift towards a legalistic approach influenced the development of child protection systems in England as well as in Australia. Leading academics and eminent practitioners were invited from England to address the Australian social workers in child protection practice. Consequently, both countries shared ideas and developments in interagency practice. There was a simultaneous exploration of how to manage cases, as well as a sharing of experience of similar problems. In both countries there were many underlying, unanswered questions that have now become part of the contemporary child protection discourse.

Secondary victimization

An important area of scrutiny is whether the nature of the intervention, investigation and continued involvement in family life is in the best interests of a child and its family, or whether the process itself creates 'secondary victimization' (Blagg and Stubbs 1988; Wattam 1992; Myers 1994; Thorpe 1994; O' Hagan and Dillenburger 1995; King 1997). Has the child protection system obtained necessary legal and forensic evidence at the cost of other considerations such as a therapeutically measured service (Wattam 1992; Buckley *et al.* 1997), or has it produced what Conte (1984: 260) identified as 'system induced trauma'?

The immediate period after a disclosure of abuse is made can be a difficult time for all concerned. Interagency communication will need to have entered its initial phase of information exchange to help assess the past and current circumstances surrounding the disclosure. The manner and speed of this action will depend upon the severity and nature of the allegation and the time, place and person to whom the allegation was made. It is well documented in child protection literature that the initial period after a disclosure of abuse is fraught with potential difficulties. If additional investigations of the alleged abuse have to be made it is likely that there will be numerous interviews of the family and child, all of which can result in further victimization of the child *and* the family.

This trauma maybe induced indirectly as the result of insensitive management, due to a lack of professional understanding and skills. A child may be asked to submit to questioning or medical examination that they had not anticipated. Alternatively, after a disclosure has been made, the professionals involved may recommend that a father leave the home, to the shock of the whole the family. These examples are not uncommon, although every effort is made to prevent unnecessary trauma. Such events are not new and contemporary joint services are developing ways to better prioritize and categorize factors involved in child sexual abuse so as to reduce such occurrences. Conte (1984) has suggested that rigorous evaluative data may help rectify this problem.

Secondary victimization has also become more apparent as reports of child abuse in foster care have come to light. Professional management and regular review of such foster placements is required to minimize any such occurrences. Informed supervision, skilled professionals and clear interagency communication are essential through all phases of the child protection process. Where interagency communications become unclear, there may be a breakdown in the management of some child protection systems. This may result in losing sight of the child and acting upon assumptions rather than accurate and timely information. The possible breakdown of communication at any point in the child protection system has led to the questioning of its effectiveness for children and families (Gough 1996; Parton *et al.* 1997; King 1997, 1999).

Impediments to partnership

In England and Wales, the Children Act 1989 set out the ethos of partnership between the state and the family in the hope that this would remedy the past problems of 'overzealous intervention' with scant regard for parental rights (Morrison 1996). It was also hoped that it would reduce the need for statutory intervention, with a stress on the prevention of child abuse. The focus of attention was to be the quality of the parent/social worker relationship. It had been suggested that parents and social workers often had different agendas during the initial stages of social work involvement. Parton *et al.* (1997: 85) refer to this, explaining that the client and the professionals usually have different 'operational perspectives'. While the social worker's aim was to obtain parental acknowledgement of the problem, the parents were looking for someone who was easy to talk to and would listen to them. Parton *et al.* (1997: 85) quote Westcott (1995: 45), who stated that 'it often appeared that clients and protection officers could not possibly be discussing the same process'. Similar findings were obtained in the research into parental attitudes after referral to statutory bodies in Western Australia, following suspected non-accidental injury to children (Lawrence and Harrison 1994). Parents in this study expressed the wish for more emotional support from both the social workers and the doctors involved in the initial investigation process.

However, further difficulties facing child protection practitioners attempting to establish and enhance a supportive relationship with the client were identified as the time available and the financial constraints under which they were expected to work. Although the Children Act 1989 quite rightly focused on working in partnership with parents, no additional resources or extra staff to enable this were provided. Furthermore, additional professional staffing and support services such as community daycare and drop-in programmes, as well as home support workers and respite care, were needed, but these were not specifically funded.

In England and Australia, legislation now attempts to ensure that the rights of children are safeguarded at the same time as respecting parental responsibility and autonomy. The challenge to contemporary practice is to come to terms with an apparently paradoxical situation. The social worker has to intervene in a mandated and often seemingly punitive way, but at the same time with the aim of empowering parents and enabling parental responsibility as a means to reduce the likelihood of harm to the child.

The dual role of child protection worker and advocate of parental empowerment need not be conflictual, but the process of achieving this working partnership with parents is, in practice, extremely difficult to attain. Family life is probably the most sacred and sensitive of relationships, thus, any kind of state intervention is fraught with difficulties. Unless this is recognized, social workers will continue to be confronted with varying degrees of defensive reaction. Ideally, the relationship should begin *before* the situation is in crisis mode. This would be more likely to happen if social workers played a more proactive role and broader social role within general welfare work.

The 'at risk' discourse and assessment model

Since the 1990s, major coalitions between children's services have been formed that focus on the identification of child abuse based on legal evidence. The development of these systems has created a further challenge to child protection practice. The domination of the socio-legal model has created phrases and images that have attained a palpable objective reality. The words 'risk' and 'child abuse' themselves have become problematic because of their different cultural reifications, which often invoke moral and politicized judgements of the phenomena (Wattam 1996; Parton *et al.* 1997). In the words of Houston and Griffiths (2000: 1), the word 'risk', 'can be likened, in the psychological terminology, to a first-order construct – or a totalizing schema – against which other constructs (such as client need) are processed or rationed'.

The completion of 'risk assessments' to identify possible abusive situations has entered the child protection discourse. Here, if there are sufficient indicators of possible abuse present then intervention is thought to be warranted. The rights of families receive a stronger focus with this change in philosophy, although this system has its critics as once again, the legal view has achieved dominance over that of the social worker role. This is reminiscent of the domination of the positivistic medical model over the social work model. A consequence of this approach has been a reduction in social workers' traditional *therapeutic* role with clients.

An imperative in child protection work is the task of differentiating 'high risk' child abuse cases from the plethora of referrals that an agency receives. As there is no consensus over the definition of 'high risk', there may be an assumption that all referrals are high risk cases. However, there is a problem in that although possible risk factors associated with child abuse have been identified, research has not yet proved a direct causal relationship between specific circumstances and confirmed abuse.

On the other hand, there is no exact science concerning the prediction of risk or abuse and this may lead to morally based decisions that are sometimes arrived at in a conservative and professionally guarded way. The 'rule of optimism' (Dingwall *et al.* 1983) may prevail and as a result a social worker will think the best of the parents and lower their threshold of concern for the child in question.

The literature has also pointed out that some decisions made in the group setting, such as those in a case conference, may result in individual members lowering their thresholds of the criteria of risk. This is said to happen because there is more security in taking a lower risk decision in groups than when having to make an individual decision (Janis 1975, 1982; Houston and Griffiths 2000).

In both of these instances, the process of decision-making based on risk assessments is open to what the literature refers to as 'statistical fallacy' – i.e. missing true cases or making false accusations. Also, there is the concomitant problem of a 'definitional fallacy', as there is no consensus on the definition of abuse. This makes it difficult to predict who will be abused, or who will abuse (Wattam 1992; Parton *et al.* 1997).

Defensive practice

With the domination of the at risk policy as described above, a further challenge facing the practitioner is how to follow policy and procedures and make defensible decisions. All institutions in society are subject to anxiety in the sense of having to justify their actions. Child protection workers (while working within an accepted, apparently objective framework) are one example of this, as they are involved in the making of individualistic and situated moral judgements. Parton (1998) has pointed out that the role of the professional is being governed at a distance by organizational and possible public sanctions.

This area of practice is haunted by past child abuse tragedies where individual faults were highlighted publicly in the media. Child protection practitioners sometimes appear to be afraid to take innovative action and in the interest of professional self-preservation, they often prefer to operate within prescribed organizational procedures. It is not uncommon to hear child protection practitioners comment that while they exercise individual discretion, they are always mindful of 'covering their backs'.

Doing well in child protection can sometimes be defined in terms of not receiving any criticism or adverse publicity, as Sanders *et al.* (1996) discovered in their research of child protection services. They reported that a respondent, who was a chairperson of an area child protection committee, remarked when asked how he knew the committee was doing a good job, 'We keep out of the papers' (Sanders *et al.* 1996: 903). So it is that concerns about risk and the fear of public sanctions and indefensible decisions affect clients and practitioners alike with their ubiquitous negativity. It is concerns about the nature of risk and its management that are said to be at the heart of many of the child protection services (Wattam 1992; Parton *et al.* 1997; Parton 1998; Houston and Griffiths 2000; Spratt *et al.* 2000).

Identification of chronic child abuse

As the child protection system is currently structured, specialized treatment centres, such as child sexual abuse clinics, are established with government funding. Their main function is the identification of child abuse and the assessment of risk. It is often concluded that the pathology lies within the family. Where abuse is substantiated, general recommendations are made for the family to adapt their childrearing practices. While a treatment centre is necessary for those who have been the victims of abuse, this represents only one aspect of a much wider community problem. The process of focusing on the identification and treatment of 'abuse' in this way decontextualizes the events (Thorpe 1994). In other words, by this that by focusing on individual pathology, there is a dismissal of the specificity of the social and economic context of the family. Thorpe (1994) identified in his research that more than half of a sample of children who were considered to be 'at risk' of neglect were from homes with lone parents with alcohol and drug problems and who were living in circumstances of poverty. Thorpe also pointed out that the evidence from his research indicated that more resources and workers with specific treatment skills that would match the needs of this group were not priority requirements. More support for parents, particularly single parents, training in alcohol and substance misuse and daycare facilities for children would have been a more economic use of resources and would have served a greater number of children who were in need.

This method of identifying individual pathology, generally referred to as the 'residual model' of service provision (Lindsey 1994), is not geared to responding to the general economic needs of disadvantaged families. As Archard (1993) points out, more children suffer from their particular social economic circumstances than from injuries suffered as a result of parental behaviour. Perhaps the negative aspects of parental behaviour could be prevented with more accessible support before things reach crisis point. It would seem, therefore, that in order to tackle the problem of child abuse it has to be understood in terms of the need for a programme of social and economic reform. Within the present system of operation, social workers are not able to alleviate the effects of poverty or provide employment or good quality accommodation.

Lindsey (1994: 190) refers to the less acute form of child abuse created at a societal level as a form of 'chronic abuse'. This is said to occur where children living in poverty, in a seemingly prosperous nation, have reduced opportunity to achieve personal success in the market economy. This is sometimes referred to as living in a 'poverty trap' and perpetuates a cycle of financial dependency on the state that in turn intensifies the 'gaze' upon this particular social group. The inclusion of all children in need and not simply those considered to be at risk of abuse would require a broadening of child welfare services and a reconceptualization of child protection. A Green Paper, *Every Child Matters* (DfES 2003), advocating a combined multi-agency approach to services for children was published in the UK in 2003.

Summary

There have been various forms of professional regulation for the prevention of neglect and the maltreatment of children. Generalist welfare programmes designed to benefit children's health, education and welfare characterized the first half of the twentieth century. This approach has also been referred to as the 'public health' model. Changes to this model were introduced in the 1960s and so began a new method of service delivery. By the late 1980s, priority service provision was aligned for the identification and treatment of 'child abuse'. The work was now set within the framework of the socio-medical model. Reliance on this positivistic approach fostered 'experts' who identified child abuse. Episodes of child abuse were seen in terms of an individual pathology that required treatment to correct, and surveillance to prevent future abuse.

This positivist method of operation began to be challenged following a number of highly publicized errors and governmental inquiry reports, especially in England. The repetition of these errors shocked the public and a backlash against social work occurred, leading to a demand for improved child protection services. The events of the child sexual abuse management scandal in Cleveland became world news in the late 1980s. The government responded by introducing new legislation and funding new research projects.

Every new public inquiry added recommendations to rectify past errors, thus adding more prescriptions to existing lengthy policies and procedures. This added to the bureaucratization of the management of child abuse.

The Children Act 1989 in England and Wales followed the events in Cleveland. Thereafter, the medical model faded from the prominence it once occupied in relation to the diagnosis of child abuse and child sexual abuse. The focus was moved away from what had been 'child abuse management' to a socio-legal perspective. Along with this shift there came the 'child protection' discourse with its greater focus on the rights of children and parents, and on working in partnership with parents.

The change of emphasis that accompanied this shift introduced a number of challenges for child protection practice. There was an emphasis on working with the police and interviewing clients for credible accounts of abuse and for the collection of forensic evidence. This decontextualization of children and their families has resulted in the diminution of the therapeutic relationship between practitioners and clients. It is criticized in the literature as a possible source of secondary victimization of children and their families and has become a major challenge to practice. Effective service delivery requires sensitive management and specialized professional attention if further trauma to the child and family are to be avoided.

During the initial period of investigation there is always the inherent dilemma of establishing a positive relationship with parents while, at the same time, conducting a mandated intervention into the private life of a family. While working in partnership with parents is a stated goal, forming this relationship in a positive and meaningful way has proven to be a further challenge to practice.

The language of the child protection discourse itself has formed another challenge. Although acknowledging the subjectivity of defining child abuse *per se*, the system continues to rely upon reified concepts of abuse. Assessments of risk are made more difficult by a lack of consensus over definitions of abuse, often making the collation of statistics regarding the incidence of child abuse unreliable. This is referred to in the literature as the 'statistical fallacy'.

Under the weight of highly prescribed risk assessments and the fear of failure to act appropriately, practitioners often make defensive decisions. In other words, some practitioners will rate all referrals as urgent and high risk to prevent being criticized. Alternatively, an underestimation of risk and possible abuse can as easily occur owing to a sense of optimism that prompts practitioners to see the best in caregivers. Once again, this opens the way to statistical fallacy in the estimation of cases of possible abuse.

The final challenge to practice discussed in this chapter stems from the positivistic framework and the tendency to overlook the social context that surrounds the incidence of abuse. This has often led to the ignoring of adverse socioeconomic circumstances that may be a major factor contributing to alleged cases of abuse. After ignoring the social context, or situations of 'chronic abuse', this same process then sets about to impose standards of childrearing practice on certain families that may be inappropriate.

4 Interagency multidisciplinary work

Introduction

This chapter begins with a discussion of the interagency multidisciplinary team approach to child protection practice. Interagency multidisciplinary work continues to be identified as a necessary, but difficult, part of intervention in child protection practice, and while this method of working continues to be favoured, it is clear from numerous official reports that review child abuse tragedies that there are attendant problems and conflicts in its operation. These problems are experienced by clients, practitioners and managers alike.

The day-to-day operation of child protection services is often the scene of interagency conflict and misunderstanding. The sheer number and variety of the various professionals involved presents a challenge to accurate and clear communication. The problems encountered in interagency working are categorized in this chapter as Level 1 or 'surface problems' and Level 2, the underlying theoretical and philosophical problems.

Level 1 problems can be experienced in a number of ways. They relate to the stresses and tensions created in the child protection system for both practitioners and clients. They also include the major interagency practice conflicts. General interagency communication difficulties are also in this first category along with specific identified barriers to interagency cooperation. All of these subdivisions of Level 1 problems are described in this chapter.

While the surface difficulties are readily identified there are other problems at a deeper level of operation that are not so readily acknowledged or understood. It could be said that there are problems behind the problems. These, the more fundamental difficulties, are referred to as Level 2 and consist of the theoretical problems. These may be created by the often competing social systems of law, welfare, economics and medicine. Each of these separate systems operates with the exclusive use of the theoretical positivistic approach to child protection. The effectiveness and appropriateness of this approach for decision-making for the social work professional is questioned.

This chapter also contains a discussion of five key criticisms of the current interagency multidisciplinary approach to child protection and welfare. These include the need for a broader and more subjectivist framework in which to work. Gaps in provision of services have been identified that require adjustment to regain a balance of facilities for all children in need. The eligibility criteria for services need to be broadened and restated. The current system has set its criteria precipitously high so as to exclude many families who have asked for assistance. It is known that most families are not even aware of what the criteria are. All of these imbalances and criticisms are outside practitioners' reach to alter. Societal, governmental and policy changes are called for to overcome the challenge of rebalancing contemporary child protection with a broader scope to include children's welfare in general. This chapter concludes by advocating the evaluation of future services. It is suggested that this evaluation and research will need a combined subjectivist and positivistic approach.

The interagency multidisciplinary approach to child protection

The initial development of interagency management of child physical abuse in the 1960s and 1970s was multidisciplinary in nature. The medical/social partnership continued to be a significant force until the mid-1980s. Since that time, inquiry reports in England have continued to maintain the multidisciplinary approach, as originally advocated and practised by the American paediatricians Kempe and Helfer (1972) for child physical abuse. Even though the medical-scientific approach that had dominated since the 1960s had lost its uncontested authority in identifying, predicting and preventing abuse, the suggested methodology of the management of child abuse and child sexual abuse remained the same (DoH 1995). The management of the problem using the interagency multidisciplinary approach continues to be the preferred method of operation in both England and Australia. This was further reinforced in England in the document *Every Child Matters* (DfES 2003). The multidisciplinary method of working was also reinforced at this time in Western Australia when the Minister for Police introduced community assistance initiatives to help reduce the occurrence of child abuse and domestic violence in Aboriginal communities in the state. These proposals were in part a response to a governmental inquiry into violence and sought as their goal to make the Aboriginal community feel safe and secure. Additionally, further initiatives are being put into place for greater coordination between the police, community development and health professionals in order to provide a more comprehensive and integrated service to children who may be victims of child abuse in Western Australia. Today, both countries continue to advocate the multidisciplinary approach to child protection.

The major formal organizations represented in the child protection system comprise social services, police, law, medicine, education and health services. These combine to form the interagency multidisciplinary core of the system. Each organization has a different role, responsibilities, perceptions and levels of knowledge relating to child abuse (Molin and Herskowitz 1986; Baglow 1990; Morrison 1990).

Since the late 1980s, legislation has empowered health and welfare personnel to intervene in the lives of children and their families in an attempt to ensure the care and protection of the child. In response to the initial rise of referrals, new legislation was set up in western countries for the greater protection of children. Over a relatively short period of time the goals of child abuse and neglect services broadened from investigations of reported cases, the protection of children and the punishment of perpetrators, to include prevention and rehabilitation services for perpetrators and the victims of abuse (Skaff 1988). All of these events have reinforced the need for an interagency multidisciplinary approach. This approach was found to be the most effective way of dealing with the reported problems, as well as coping with the increasing scope of demands being made on existing systems.

The Baglow multidimensional model

Several authors have illustrated the interagency multidisciplinary method of working and its complexity with flow diagrams (see Hallett and Birchall, 1992: 300–1). The Baglow multidimensional model (1990: 338) represents a typical interagency multidisciplinary method of case management and is depicted as a flow diagram in Figure 4.1. This model also describes stages at which problems of interagency communication might occur. By understanding the process at each stage, agencies and individuals are able to communicate with each other effectively, enhance their mutual cooperation and improve child abuse treatment outcomes. In order to understand the significance of interagency cooperation while working with families, it is essential to be aware of the possible multiple perspectives from each of the participants. Some of these may be highly emotional and personal conflicts may occur. If this happens it may impact adversely on the following stages of the treatment model. For example, if a family is told that a non-accidental injury suffered by their child will need to be referred to the social services and the police, a highly defensive reaction is not uncommon.

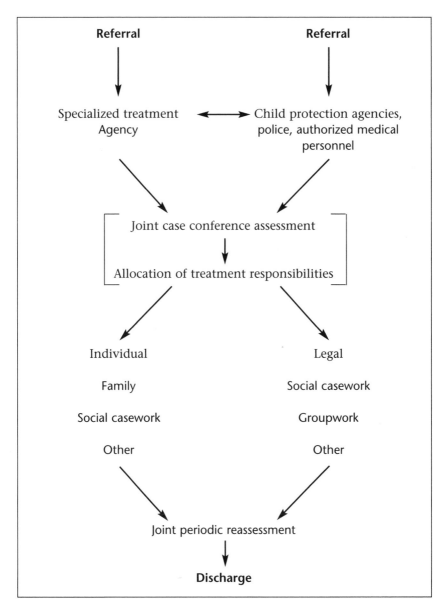

Figure 4.1 A multidimensional model for treatment of child abuse

On the left of Figure 4.1 is the input of a specialised treatment team. This may be a child guidance clinic, a hospital treatment team or a community child abuse treatment team. On the right is the input from the child protection agency, the police, or the authorized medical personnel. Cases of abuse may enter from the right or the left. However, the arrow that connects the two sides is double-headed to represent the fact that both sets of agencies are involved. It is no longer therapeutically acceptable, and in some cases unlawful, for specialist treatment teams to treat cases of child abuse alone and in isolation. Increasingly, statutory bodies are asking specialized centres for assistance. This early phase in the treatment process when agencies first begin to interact is referred to as the *cross-referral stage*. While interagency multidisciplinary models, such as the one described here, were acknowledged as necessary in the literature and in a government document in the 1970s and 1980s, the lack of adequate funding continues to remain a feature for recommended legislation in respect of child abuse treatment and prevention to the present day.

These demands upon services increased exponentially in the early 1980s. This increase in referrals was matched by a growth of services in the social, physical, emotional and legal spheres. The belief was that no single agency had pre-eminent responsibility in the assessment of child abuse in general and child sexual abuse specifically. The principle underpinning this approach was that a coordinated and holistic service would provide a coherent resource for children and families and not one which would be confused and disparate. It was also believed that assessments and contributions brought to a case conference would bring a rigour to the proceedings and should therefore produce a fairer evaluation of the circumstances (David 1994).

Additionally, it was felt that the multidisciplinary 'working together' method was of value to the practitioner in terms of lessening the tensions of difficult work and as a source of support that would ease the burden of responsibility (Hallett and Birchall 1992; Hallett 1993; David 1994). Further to these ideas about the value of working together, O'Hagan (1989) reminds us that an often forgotten tenet in the professional code of ethics is the duty to liaise, cooperate and work with other agencies that are also serving the clients. O'Hagan and Anthony *et al.* (1988) point out that the ethical code requires that much thinking and preparation has to be done before embarking upon any action on behalf of clients.

As the overall awareness of the complexity of the problem of child abuse grew, there followed a mammoth response in the political and professional arenas with a concomitant burgeoning of new areas of specialism in medicine, law, social work and education. These professional groups were now expected to work together, often for the first time, in the management and treatment of children who had been sexually abused. Some of these professionals were already working in interdisciplinary teams, others operated in separate and unrelated agencies. Many of these professionals had never previously worked in a team. Some professions had histories of being hierarchical and authoritarian in structure and others were more egalitarian and regularly engaged in democratically arrived at decisions.

After the introduction of the multidisciplinary approach for the identification and management of child abuse, the implications for those working with child sexual abuse became more apparent. However, as Elliot and Merrill (1961) have pointed out, roles that arose under one set of circumstances were often inadequate to meet the exigencies of another set. Before the 1960s, the various professional groups in child health and welfare operated primarily in their own spheres of influence. With the development and growth of child protection teams there were both legislative and informal mandates to work together in both England and Australia. Role expectations needed to be clarified and adapted accordingly.

Despite these negative aspects, the various agency and professional links that were formed in those early days have continued with improved services in the contemporary setting. Prescriptions for working together now exist in government documents (e.g. DoH 1991b) and in the spirit of those whose daily job it is to respond meaningfully to child abuse referrals. While today's child protection services have accomplished improved systems of communication in interagency and multidisciplinary work, many problems remain.

Inherent difficulties of interagency multidisciplinary work

The contemporary interagency multidisciplinary arrangements in the management of child sexual abuse have revealed inherent difficulties that may profoundly affect the well-being of clients and the work of practitioners. There are concerns that indicate undesirable outcomes are possible, resulting in forms of continued maltreatment of children and distraught parents who may be falsely assessed (Conte 1984; Blagg and Stubbs 1988; Myers 1994).

There is also the possibility of fatigue or 'burnout' among practitioners whose daily job it is to resolve dilemmas about child abuse. The number and variety of different professionals involved exacerbates these possible negative outcomes. For example, each of these professions may have its own individual perspectives on child sexual abuse, and this can result in different professionals having different definitions of child sexual abuse and different assumptions as regards treatment and prevention.

Areas of potential conflict in child protection management are being addressed on a routine and individual basis in a professional manner and this continues to be a relatively under-researched area (Scott 1997). It has been estimated that in the UK there may be up to 72 different professionals involved in a single family's network when there are suspicions of child abuse (Reder *et al.* 1993: 65). Furthermore, professionals from differing backgrounds can also have different theoretical frameworks about the nature of childhood itself, as well as views on the rights of parents. This may result in disagreements as to whether to intervene at all when abuse is suspected. This can be complicated further by the opinions of concerned referrers, primary caregivers, children and their families.

While many of these problems of interagency communication have been addressed in practice, other underlying problems remain. It is possible to categorize these problems into a hierarchy of surface problems at Level 1 and underlying theoretical and philosophical problems at Level 2. These classifications are discussed in the next two sections.

Level 1: surface problems in the interagency multidisciplinary approach

It can be appreciated that interagency multidisciplinary management problems may occur at a variety of interacting levels. Practitioners and managers are both subject to these problems and need to keep an active dialogue to resolve them as they arise. All of these identified areas need to be accountably addressed by professionals in order to interact satisfactorily in the lives of children and their families. If not effectively addressed, conflicts may arise within the child protection system that can generate enormous frustrations, and such dynamics have potentially serious implications not only for clients but also for practitioners.

Tensions and stresses

The literature has pointed out that the presence of anxiety as a highly charged phenomenon can exist throughout the child protection process for families and practitioners alike. The Baglow multidimensional model depicted the tensions that may exist for practitioners at times of cross-referral of clients in the interagency coordination and collaboration process. Additionally, there is ample reference in the literature to the near-crisis state of anxiety that exists for parents when they first meet professionals to discuss possible child abuse (Lawrence and Harrison 1994; Morrison 1996; Parton *et al.* 1997). Baglow's (1990) purposeful discussion and acknowledgement of the stresses that existed for families and professionals also clarified that it was the responsibility of the agency to offer support and appropriate systems of management for these stresses. It has been suggested that if the anxieties generated in the professional in this process were left unattended, these matters might have led to defensive and dysfunctional practice (Morrison 1996).

Baglow reminded us that problems in the course of assessment and treatment can and do arise even in routine referrals that are not ostensibly concerned with abuse. For example, a specialist treatment centre regularly receives referrals about children and behaviour problems, many of which are resolved with appropriate assessment and advice. Although a child may have been referred initially in this way as a 'non-abuse' problem, there may be times during assessment or treatment when child abuse is subsequently revealed. In these cases the management becomes even more complex, exacerbating tension.

The literature notes that exposure to matters of child abuse itself is stressful for the professionals involved (Hallett and Birchall 1992; Stanley and Goddard 1993). This stress is cumulative and so will increase with time unless resolved as it occurs. Baglow (1990) has suggested that it is advisable to be aware of specific interagency contact points ahead of time so as to minimize potential conflicts and stress.

When parents become stressed their ability to engage in the process and form any therapeutic partnership for the benefit of their child is hindered. Prepared guidelines for interagency coordination and case management that are created to take account of potential crisis points will help to meet these eventualities. Such organizational mechanisms need to be designed and tested to avoid exposing clients and practitioners to potentially insensitive or inappropriate stresses.

Practice conflicts

Scott (1997) identified three main categories of interagency multidisciplinary conflict. These are as follows.

The first refers to 'gatekeeping', a term familiar in the child protection discourse, used in this instance to describe the reluctance of an overworked child protection service to accept referrals from other organizations. In such a situation, some referrers may overemphasize the negative aspects of a case to have it accepted. On the other hand, the overworked authority may discount the extent of the problems presented, as it believes that exaggerations are being made when, in fact, they may be being presented accurately.

The second category exists in what Scott refers to as 'dispositional disputes'. This is where a conflict occurs between a statutory agency and the police or a hospital. The legal disposition awarded to the case by the statutory agency is thought to be an inadequate level of statutory intervention by the other agencies. Scott believes that this reflects a 'philosophical difference'. This sort of conflict can occur in a children's hospital when hospital staff think that the seriousness of the injuries to an infant warrants a court order for formal post-discharge monitoring. It may be that the statutory service decides otherwise and plans a voluntary association with the family. This can in turn prove extremely frustrating for the hospital staff and would reflect adversely on the quality of the interagency relationship. This can result in hospital staff feeling that their opinion is undervalued, producing resentment and possibly a refusal to participate in further child abuse cases.

The third category referred to by Scott is that of 'domain disputes'. This type of conflict may occur where there is a degree of overlap of responsibilities between two agencies with a consequent blurring of boundaries. For example, in the 1980s, during the initial establishment of interagency teams, there were insufficient guidelines for managing cases of child sexual abuse. The role of the police sometimes overlapped with the responsibilities of a hospital-based, child sexual abuse clinic. On several occasions the police were known to bring children to the hospital in the early hours of the morning for interviews and examinations for possible sexual assault. Social workers and the appropriate medical staff had to be called in solely for this purpose. In several of these cases there was no history of recent assault and no immediate forensic evidence to warrant emergency intervention. Apart from being potentially traumatizing to bring children to an emergency room in a hospital in the middle of the night, it would have been less stressful and more convenient if the police had planned their appointment during routine clinic hours.

Communication difficulties

Buckley *et al.* (1997) identified similar problems in interagency multi-disciplinary child protection work that closely resemble the points mentioned by Scott (1997). Buckley's team identified three areas of potential conflict with regard to interagency communication, and they refer to these as 'structural factors', warning that they can negatively affect interagency working together. The first is 'delays of one sort or another' (1997: 121). A great deal of frustration can be experienced in interagency work when one agency's work does not easily coordinate with another. As in the example given above, the police who wanted the children interviewed in the early hours were keen to pursue a suspect and would have preferred the work to be done as soon as possible. Matching the priorities of various agencies can be a challenge. If it is the mandated task of the agency to deal with emergency matters it is imperative that they are organized to do so. The inherent slowness of some agencies, such as the legal system, does cause dissatisfaction to clients and other services as treatment issues are sometimes left unresolved (Wattam 1992).

The second area referred to by Buckley *et al.* (1997: 122–3), concerns issues of feedback and communication. Staff changes, the busy schedule of workers and, more directly, a lack of organizational mechanisms to coordinate these issues and make provision to ensure necessary communication can all cause problems. In such instances it would seem to be the agency's responsibility to ascertain if the communication procedure was being completed and to install helpful mechanisms for its completion. Examples of such deficits in communication as referred to above were also noted in the report prepared by Lord Laming after the Victoria Climbié Inquiry (Laming 2003).

In addition, the exchange of information between adult services and child-based agencies is a well-known area of difficulty. One of the problems arises from the fact that childcare agencies hold the rights of the child to be paramount, whereas the adult services feel bound by confidentiality to clients only. Buckley *et al.* (1997) have identified the principle of confidentiality as one of the main reasons for difficulties concerning feedback and communication. An example of this may occur in a community-based maternity hospital. The hospital may refuse to exchange information based on their adult client's right to confidentiality. This may occur even though a child-based statutory agency has serious concerns about the well-being of the child who is about to be born. In such situations government intervention may be needed to rectify the situation.

In Western Australia, the lack of authority to exchange information in respect of child protection issues has been rectified by the Child Welfare Amendment Act 2002. This allows the Department for Community Development and other government agencies to request and disclose information that is or is likely to have relevance to the health, safety or welfare of a child. In addition, this legislation declares that the best interest of the child is paramount, as has been stated in England and Wales in the Children Act 1989.

The third area identified by Buckley *et al.* refers to problems relating to professional roles, status and responsibilities. These authors found that most professionals in the child protection network were clear about their roles; however, they were unsure about their *status* in the child protection network and uncertain about the *value* of their information to such proceedings as case conferences. Some child protection practitioners felt that too much responsibility was placed on them in their ascribed role.

Barriers to cooperation

There are many possible barriers to interagency cooperation. Among them are the five Stevenson (1989b) identified as major barriers to interagency cooperation. She summaries these areas of potential difficulties as follows:

1   the multitude of varying structures and systems involved in the child protection network;
2   questions concerning the value of exchanging information and confidentiality implications;

3   status and perceived power variations and responsibility across professions, which are further complicated by gender, age, ethnic origin, employment, income etc.;
4   variations in professional and organizational priorities concerning child abuse issues; and
5   varying staff concerns about whether it is to their benefit or worth cooperating.

It is evident that neither verbal or written agreements can ensure that interagency cooperation will automatically occur. Neither law nor report recommendations, in themselves, necessarily create cooperation without attention being paid to the specific needs of those individuals asked to implement them. There may be a covert reluctance and concerns by some agencies to comply with mutually agreed upon procedures. In these cases, a continuing dialogue is necessary to satisfactorily resolve the matter at issue. The attainment of cooperation and goodwill with other agencies in the interagency process is considered to be part of an ongoing process of interagency communication.

Level 2: underlying theoretical problems

There are underlying 'problems behind the problems' that often prevent effective interagency cooperation in the management of child protection. These problems are mainly theoretical and philosophical in nature. Many of the Level 1, surface difficulties encountered in the interagency multi-disciplinary approach are the practical manifestations of underlying problems. Some of these stem from the competing areas of children's and parents' rights, state intervention in family life, legal constraints, politics and the socioeconomic marginalization of poverty (Lyon and Kouloumpos-Lenares 1987; Smart 1990; Fox Harding 1991a, 1991b; Birchall and Hallet 1995; Wattam 1996; Buckley et al. 1997; Scott 1997). Even if these problems are given attention at a surface level, the effectiveness of services will continue to falter unless the underlying theoretical and philosophical principles are addressed. Foremost among such difficulties is the challenge of achieving a balance between the objective and subjective approaches in child protection management. This will be discussed further below, along with other often unacknowledged problems.

Objectivity and decision-making

In England, attempts to enhance and rationalize the child protection system became a theme after each child abuse inquiry (Reder et al. 1993).

The proliferation of further procedures such as risk assessments for the identification of possible abuse and the trend to introduce systems of checks and balances, such as auditing social workers, highlighted a shift towards the legal control of child protection. The trend of the increased policies and procedures was referred to by Howe (1992) as the 'bureaucratisation' of social work. All of these attempts to rationalize and systematize decision-making were the result of identified errors stemming from the operation of the socio-medical model (Howitt 1992). Thereafter, the scrutiny of social work decision-making was shifted to the legal discourse in order to ensure that *defensible* decisions were made. New performance standards were also introduced into the child protection discourse and became known as the 'new managerialism' (King 1997). However, the fact that decision-making remained within a strictly scientific objectivist model meant that underlying paradoxes remained unresolved.

Lawyers were now seen as central figures in case conference decision-making processes. Whereas previously it was only the clients who were under the 'legal gaze', social workers were now also subject to the legal discourse (Parton 1991). The investigation of allegations of child abuse was dominated by the pursuit of evidence (Wattam 1992). Decisions were being made on the basis of what was considered to be 'objective evidence'. However, sometimes, where there was not sufficient evidence, the case would not be pursued even though the child or the parent reported that abuse had occurred. On the other hand, even where there may have been clear evidence of a crime against a child, there may have been a moral judgement by the social workers concerned not to proceed any further with formal action. This could have been because they deemed that the child felt that the matter was settled and the family had acted summarily to end the abuse and prevent its reoccurrence. This illustrates the dilemma between what is considered to be a crime against a child and child abuse. The legally pursuable case will sometimes dictate whether a crime has occurred against a child, but not whether child abuse has occurred. Once again, this highlights the dilemma that results from the adoption of a strictly objectivist model and the confusion that exists in regard to definitions.

Deciding if there are sufficient grounds to establish official 'standards of proof' resides often with the person who is mandated to review the situation. An example of this is on record in a child sexual abuse clinic. Interviews in this clinic were conducted jointly by a social worker and a physician. A 10-year-old female 'client' on this occasion was accompanied by her cousin of the same age. The cousin had been encouraged to attend as moral support for the client who was said to be 'shy'. As the interview commenced, the cousin exhorted the client to be 'frank with the ladies' and tell them 'the truth' to make things better. She went on to say that she understood, as this had happened to her once. She then described how her grandfather had shown her pornographic videos. The interviewers were now alarmed, as there appeared to be *two* cases to investigate. The cousin then described that she had told her mother, who had become angry with the grandfather and told him to stop it and never do it again. The emphatic tone with which she told the story also illustrated the fact that she had thought that her mother had done a good job. As a result she knew she was safe and that abuse would not reoccur. Attention returned to the original client for the remainder of the interview, but a decision was made to discuss the cousin's disclosure with her mother at a later stage. This was done and the mother gave an identical account of the story and said that the matter was now closed. A moral judgement was made in this instance that there was no case to report to the police.

Social workers make risk assessment decisions within a normative framework – that is, within statistically established figures of what may be expected – when assessing referrals. The normative framework also includes the practitioner's general overall knowledge with an assumed objectivity. Decisions are made based on this assumed objectivity with regard to the accumulation of research knowledge about abuse, practice knowledge, and ideas about current cultural childrearing patterns. Decisions are also made based upon ideas of what constitutes 'normal' parenting: 'The illusion and pretence of objectivity and neutrality serves the interests of those empowered by the status quo and the bias in professional decision making' (Fineman 1989: 45). Added to this, in cases where there are degrees of uncertainty, there will be a moral assessment based on assumed cultural and community standards and on the information available relating to the family's 'total' circumstances (Dingwall *et al.* 1983; King 1997; Parton *et al.* 1997).

Assumed objectivity is now open to question, and practitioner bias may be seen to be a problem at the heart of practice. The assumption of objectivity is also questioned by the feminist critique, as it has been associated with gender (Fineman 1989). In this sense, objectivity has been associated with rational masculinity, whereas the subjective has been associated with the feminine and natural (Smart 1990).

Another questioning of professional assumed objectivity is reported by Dingwall *et al.* (1983). These authors refer to the 'rule of optimism' underlying social workers' assessments, meaning that they operate with the assumption that parents generally love their children and will do their best for them. Social workers have been accused of a discriminatory bias in arriving at decisions in this way, and as a result are placed under pressure as they are expected, by their agency, and also by the law, to make what are considered to be defensible decisions. There is an expectation on social workers to retain so-called objectivity.

This raises the issue of what is regarded as 'normal' and 'abnormal'. Various authors have defined 'normality' for the purposes of their research, usually based on correlational studies: for example, correlating socio-economic backgrounds of families with deviant behaviour. The results of this kind of research are then extrapolated to apply to the population as a whole. However, because two phenomena regularly occur together does not necessarily mean that one causes the other. In any case, there is never a one-to-one correlation between two types of behaviour when one is concerned with personal characteristics. King (1997) points out that statistical studies are of little assistance to the practitioner as they can only provide an indication of the *probability* of certain events happening. This is where the practitioner has to make a moral judgement using the normative framework as a guideline. In other words, the assessment has to be made combing both the objectivistic and the subjectivist perspectives.

One of the challenges of child protection practice is to accommodate both perspectives. The struggle between objectivism and subjectivism is a part of everyday life; as when interpersonal conflicts occur when two friends view a situation differently. This same challenge confronts the practitioner who has to make defensible positivistic decisions about incidents that are socially constructed, such as child abuse.

King (1997) refers this challenge to as a paradox in the social work system. The social worker is being put into the impossible dilemma of having to make scientific, positivist judgements, while at the same time being aware of the social construction of abuse. Even science itself has been found to be confusing and unconvincing when it comes to the specific questions involved in the identification of and intervention in child abuse (Beck 1992). It appears that society has in many ways now lost the confidence that it once placed in the expert, whether we are speaking of social workers or scientists (Giddens 1991). Even so, there is an implicit acceptance in society that there is a hierarchy of status among professions. The medical and legal professions have traditionally been dominant. Social work, a relatively new profession with an eclectic knowledge base, is often regarded as the 'Cinderella' service. Clearly more attention needs to be focused on enhancing the status of social work. Movements in this direction are already in hand with extensive postgraduate training now available and the establishment of an all-graduate profession.

There have been open and vigorous criticisms of the decision-making process regarding the phenomenon of child abuse in the child protection system. The establishment of parents' rights groups reflects a lack of confidence in the system. It is also reflects the increased reliance on the socio-legal discourse and the inclusion of self-auditing and regulation of the new managerialism in social work (Jones and May 1995; King 1997). Both of these trends are questioned as part of a move towards a defensive demonstration of accountability and the need for rigorously professional practice (King 1997; Parton *et al.* 1997).

This questioning of the scientific method has informed the current debates on social issues in general (Beck *et al.* 1994). The critique of the scientific perspective has been described as a 'late modern scepticism' in which positivism has been devalued (Beck 1992). Social work was particularly vulnerable to these criticisms with its public and statutory role in the management of child abuse, a social construction that still demanded to be defined within a positivist framework. With a growing list of child abuse tragedies, trust in the social worker declined and the reflexive practice audit was developed to demonstrate that a good job was being done.

The new managerialism in Australia introduced quality assurance procedures and self-evaluative exercises. Unfortunately, this coincided with an economic downturn and reduced funding for services. There was pressure on social workers from both clients and the administrators of government funds to demonstrate that 'quality' work was being accomplished.

The social scientific premises on which the child protection system of risk assessment, abuse identification and intervention had been based were not questioned and the language of social work decision-making was left unchallenged. As the managerial system implied, a rational approach to achieve effectiveness carries with it the danger in a human service organization that it might overlook or conceal harmful consequences.

Currently, ministers in England are in a position of reviewing 5000 civil cases where children had been removed from their families on the basis of a positivistic diagnosis of Munchausen's Syndrome by Proxy. The removal of these children occurred over a 15-year period and the professional who made the judgements has subsequently been discredited. This scenario raises many issues including whether these children would have been categorized in this way if more subjective factors had been taken into account.

Plans in the UK to redevelop child protection systems have now been put into place. However, the day-to-day work of statutory child protection will continue to be a mixture of official procedures and individual professional discretion. Although the refocusing of child protection work towards a more subjectivist approach would appear to lead to more accurate assessments, the practitioner is still faced with the need to assess whether a child is at risk of harm, and has to make a judgement accordingly. Parton *et al.* (1997) refer to this decision-making activity as 'risk insurance', which clearly is different from traditional judgements made on the basis of collating objective evidence. This is developed further by Parton (1998) who argues that the risks assessed by child protection practitioners are virtual in the sense that they are not strictly objectifiable.

It is suggested that 'ambiguity' and 'uncertainty' characterize the subjectivist approach and also most assessments of child abuse (Parton 1998: 23). Parton suggests that this should be recognized by practitioners as a central point in their work. This means that social workers must be prepared for uncertainty rather than experiencing anxiety when confronted with an ambiguous situation. Parton considers that social work practitioners need to rethink the way in which they establish relationships with their clients and should attempt to rediscover the perspective of uncertainty and ambiguity in their work.

Organizational systems in child protection

King (1997, 1999) proposes that the underlying problems of unresolved issues and lack of congruence in the management of child abuse are best understood in terms of the 'closed systems theory'. Closed systems refer to the social systems of such institutions as law, medicine, economics and politics. Each operates according to its own procedures and is dependent upon the others for authoritative statements, but this is not done in a simple input-output manner. Each system can only communicate in terms of its own discourse and will only understand information that is similarly codified. Thus each system, which consists of its own body of knowledge and understandings, becomes increasingly independent and autonomous. It is this closed functional perspective that often makes working together in the multidisciplinary team problematic. Social work is not a closed system but it does need to coordinate and collaborate its functions within the frameworks of medicine, education and law.

The difficulty of working together is further exacerbated by the fact that a closed system does not communicate in terms of morality. Moral judgements as to what is good or bad, right or wrong, are not in the parlance of these closed systems. They do not take heed of individual moralities. Individuals in general develop their own moral code and each generation and each group develops its own code so there is no absolute sense of what is right or wrong. In this sense, some would support the idea that even the scientist cannot be a totally detached observer of nature.

The problem of connecting a particular individual's life to society entails ensuring that the voice of an individual or group is not oppressed by the majority in the democratic process (Heffner 1960). The government of the day would usually claim to be operating within an acceptable moral code, although this is often difficult for various groups to accept. The fact that closed systems do not heed the moral discourse is often seen to be immoral and unjust (King 1997).

However, there is some benefit to be obtained when a system does not become involved in questions of morality, provided that the system concerned is aware of the need to involve the subjective endeavours of other groups. The benefits of a closed system may be seen, for example, in the case of medicine: doctors cannot afford to question the worthiness of a patient before deciding to provide adequate treatment. Once again this illustrates the need to balance the objective and the subjective processes in decision-making.

Where cases of child abuse and child sexual abuse are reported and confirmed, the legal discourse has shifted to accommodate the evidence, feelings and wishes of children (Wattam 1992; McKenna 1999). However, this assistance is still defined within the legalist framework for the gathering of evidence. The rule of law continues to take precedence at the expense of other considerations, such as the possible need for therapeutic intervention on behalf of the child and family, as noted above. Even though adaptations have occurred the procedures continue to focus primarily on legalistic mechanisms.

The implication of this in child protection formulations is that social workers have mainly incorporated the objectivist approach within their practice. However, the underlying premises of this analysis have been questioned (Parton *et al.* 1997). Given the present state of knowledge, the scientific model alone is not sufficient to understand the complex nature of child abuse. Also, it is generally acknowledged that, as child abuse is a social construction, decision-making takes the form of risk assessments with the attendant problems that accompany this method. Moreover, closed systems do not have a full human perspective on the individuals with whom they interact. At any one time such systems regard only that facet of a person that informs their own organization. As King (1997: 143) comments, 'each solution providing system is able to see only part of what is recognized by society as "the problem"'.

Currently, in England the Green Paper *Every Child Matters* (DfES 2003) seeks to reorganize children's services by grouping together the departments of education, health and children's social services into one localized 'children's trust'. Some considerable work will need to be done in order to accommodate the reorganization and integration of these specific and unique organizations into one department. Otherwise there could be insurmountable problems as traditionally each organization has had its own aims and objectives. Clearly there has been a need for change and provided that the new blend of services receives proper support, the broadening of organizational scope to a general welfare goal should prove to be of benefit to those in need. As far as future developments are concerned, this broadened scope will allow for a moderation of the strictly positivistic stance. The interagency multidisciplinary method of working will continue to be the favoured method of organization and will be at the forefront of the new services.

Key criticisms of current interagency multidisciplinary work

Key criticisms of contemporary interagency multidisciplinary work centre on five major areas. These criticisms have been supported by a number of authors (e.g. Parton 1998; Payne 1998; Morris and Shepherd 2000; Spratt *et al.* 2000).

The need for subjectivism

It is suggested that a broader focus should include a greater awareness of the-subjectivist approach in all agencies. For this to work, this particular perspective will need to be reflected in the aims and objectives of the various professions. For social work, this represents a return to the traditional core values and skills of the profession, with a strong focus on the therapeutic relationship in service delivery.

Further exploration of the current mechanisms in interagency communication may mean that the structures that are now in place and that operate within a positivistic framework may require a policy shift among all agencies to accommodate a more subjectivist approach. Within the strictly positivistic model, as applied in the health and legal services, the screening of clients has been so rigorously employed that child protection practitioners have been seen in the 'expert' role as decision-makers in matters of child-rearing and child abuse. Although this does occur from time to time in the social work field, it is more commonly experienced in the legal and medical professions. For example, the social worker's more subjectivist angle would complement the positivistic one usually adopted by the medical profession rather than being in opposition to it. Hence, when a medical practitioner has diagnosed the physical signs of possible abuse, the social worker's more subjectivist approach to the problem should be given equal credibility.

The authoritative role adopted by some professionals has been primarily paradoxical in its application of scientific rules to human behaviour. With our present knowledge, the evidence indicates that it is not always possible to be so precise when predicting human behaviour. A total reliance on the strictly scientific method can often inhibit clear communication and partnership with clients and professionals.

A more subjectivist approach would place a phenomenological emphasis on situated judgements and take into account the personal experience of the client, as well as of other agencies. This approach would allow for greater plurality, but without total relativism. It would allow for a humanistic perspective, taking into account the fact that people are potentially self-determining and able to construct their own phenomenological environments. This would also be more likely to enhance communication with clients and between the professionals from different agencies.

The current dilemmas facing the child welfare services should be addressed by each agency as a priority. The resolution of these dilemmas would suggest the adoption of a more subjectivist approach by all agencies in child welfare. The planning of policy and services to accommodate this shift would require a reordering of political and governmental priorities and resources. In order to implement a more subjectivist approach toward clients, it would be necessary for practitioners to have organizational support to offer and implement this modified method of practice. This shift of approach would require total commitment from the child welfare agencies, with governmental backing, for the new philosophy to be successfully administered. A policy change of this dimension would need to be clearly stated and would also need to demonstrate how such a change of emphasis could be accommodated within current legislative guidelines.

In England, the need for the reorganization of child and family services into a programme with a more universally-based philosophy has been recognized. As previously mentioned, a major proposed change to reform and improve services for children by combining education, health and social services on one site has been introduced. Changes to infant welfare services were introduced in Western Australia in 2002 with the establishment of an early intervention programme for the Aboriginal community, providing extra resources for infant health and maternal well-being. This programme has been introduced as a partial response to a government inquiry into child abuse and domestic violence among Aboriginals in Western Australia (Gordon 2002).

Gaps in services

Child Protection: Messages From Research (DoH 1995) has been criticized for the continuation of the inherent bias of defining children 'in need' as those primarily at risk and so missing an opportunity to set out a reorganization of welfare services (Wattam 1996). The policy components in child protection management – of prevention, investigation and treatment (Sanders *et al.* 1996) – are all intrinsically linked. New directives concerning priorities would need to be established to broaden the current focus. In England, this would involve a broadening of service delivery to include not only child protection cases, but also children and families 'in need', as specified in the Children Act 1989.

The legalistic child protection system can mean that many families who suffer from economic hardship and minimal social support do not receive the help they need. Many of these families may be socially marginalized or have children with special health needs, and therefore qualify for assistance as defined by the Children Act 1989. Despite the development of legislation in England that upholds the recognition of the special category of need for children, some families have continued to be unaware of this declaration. Its potential use to develop imaginative preventive programmes in disadvantaged communities appears to have been missed. This is probably because most agencies did not have the necessary resources to provide even a full service for children with identified special needs, so they are sometimes reluctant to advertize the new provision.

It is now hoped that the restructuring of services as suggested by *Every Child Matters* (DfES 2003) will remedy situations such as this. The proposals in this document set out the largest reorganization of children's services for decades. The new system was introduced into 35 local authorities in 2003 and is planned to be established in every English local authority by 2006. While the aims and goals of the reordered services have been broadly welcomed, fears remain that lack of financial support and a scarcity of programmes will continue to fail to make provision for children in need as well as those who need protection. However, the Green Paper has acknowledged many of the major challenges that complicate the proposed changes and has set out positive responses to help in the realignment of the previous care systems. Some of these new proposals include 'Sure Start' programmes for preschool children, extended daycare, parent support services, parenting classes and a national parents' helpline. The government has also recognized the need to improve the training and retention of childcare professional and volunteers. To achieve this it is introducing a new workforce strategy for all childcare workers, encouraging higher standards of recruitment, education and practice skills.

Eligibility criteria for services

Child welfare services need to be more inclusive in providing family support and treatment. Under many present systems, an ever-increasing number of families are becoming the subject of investigation, with fewer receiving the practical supportive treatment they need. Recently, the contemporary child protection system has been criticized because of the relatively narrow, positivistic and punitive framework that has become its core (Marneffe 1996; Parton *et al.* 1997; Houston and Griffiths 2000; Spratt *et al.* 2000). It was also said that many children and families were primarily being screened to mesh with the judicial system – that is, they are only eligible for assistance once abuse has occurred or they are deemed to be high risk cases (Wattam 1992).

Under the current system, the needs of those families who may require help in health and social matters before any abuse has occurred are disregarded. There is little scope for preventive work and early intervention in the classical child protection scenario. Lack of funds, resources and understaffing in many areas has dramatically increased workloads and this has made the filtering system more acceptable than otherwise it might have been. Additionally, the ever-broadening definitions of abuse and children at risk of possible abuse has further increased the workload of services and limited the criteria for eligibility for them. There is a need for child welfare systems to be reorganized to correct this imbalance.

Often, families are said to have little understanding of the eligibility criteria to receive services. Even when eligible for help within the child protection system, families are sometimes moved from one section to another without the process being explained to them (Morris and Shepherd 2000). For many, involvement in the child protection process is seen alienating, and this often applies to clients and practitioners alike as they experience a distancing from the decision-making process.

It is not uncommon to hear clients say that they had contacted social services for help previously, but had formed the impression that no one would assist them unless there was a crisis. Many families who requested help at an early stage of their concerns failed to understand why the criteria for eligibility for services were set so precipitously high. A possible reason was that the child protection system had been fashioned in the wake of child abuse 'worst case scenarios'. The legislation, policy and procedures in contemporary practice have been so organized as to prevent tragedies from reoccurring by prior identification of risk factors. Where the funding for services had been cut they have tended to concentrate their efforts on crisis management (Reder *et al.* 1993).

Imbalance in the system

Acknowledgement should be made that the rebalancing of the system goes beyond the remit of the individual practitioner. It would seem to be even beyond the remit of area child protection committees in England. These committees are charged with the role of interagency coordination of child protection services and have a duty to provide services in all three areas of investigation, prevention and treatment. It would not be unreasonable to expect them to address the need to reorder priorities for a more equitable distribution of resources. Moreover, it would seem that underlying societal values ought to be debated and a political commitment made to reshape the services.

The competing approaches represented in the multidisciplinary systems of the law, state welfare distribution, children's and families' rights and the state's right to intervene in family life all need to be conceptually re-examined and reordered. Many of these issues are currently being addressed in England as recommended via *Every Child Matters* (DfES 2003). One of the newly-stated recommendations in this document is the replacement of area child protection committees with local safeguarding boards that will have statutory powers to integrate key services for children.

Research and evaluation considerations

The 1980s was a time of turbulence between interdisciplinary multiagency teams and the public concerning the management of child sexual abuse. The organization and functioning of services was criticized both by the public and official inquiry reports. The newly-created interagency multidisciplinary services set up in the 1980s in England and Australia to manage child abuse represented the early days of development and were not based on adequate research (O'Hagan 1989). This may have been because, as many authors have now acknowledged, services at this time for the management of child abuse were in their infancy (Sgroi 1982; O'Hagan 1989; Vizard *et al.* 1995).

Numerous authors have said that the organization of services has been guided more by inquiry reports, which exposed mistakes, than by practice-based valid research (Parton 1991; Hallet and Birchall 1992; Howitt 1992; Wattam 1992; Reder *et al.* 1993; Buckley *et al.* 1997; Parton *et al.* 1997). Child protection systems appear to have followed an evolutionary progression along a path constructed and reconstructed from recommendations following public notoriety over what were considered to be serious professional errors (Howitt 1992).

The problems that arose thereafter in interagency multidisciplinary working have highlighted the need for further research in this area (Buckley *et al.* 1997). The rise in numbers, the expansion of definitional issues and the conflicts and dilemmas posed by children's and parents' rights groups revealed the difficulties of working together in this complex field of endeavour. Much of the early research in the field of child sexual abuse traditionally focused on the quantitative approach, involving surveys of large populations in an attempt to come to terms with the extent and nature of the problem. More often than not, this involved the use of correlational techniques to investigate relationships between the incidence of child abuse and personal and familial characteristics. This traditional statistical approach was also used to predict generalized probabilities. Neither of these methods of research proved to be of value to the practitioner faced with an individual case (King 1997). This research was neither practice based nor action oriented (O'Hagan 1989).

Many of the large-scale survey designs into incidence and prevalence treated the subject of abuse as a reified, actual commodity in an attempt to describe the size of the problem, and ignored the context of the phenomenon. A great deal of the early research did not recognize that child abuse was a social construction. This may have been because it was assumed that the scientific method employed in the physical sciences would be equally valid when applied to the social sciences.

Much of this research adopted a strictly positivistic approach, borrowing from the physical sciences with their interest in cause and effect relationships and claiming to be value-free. Even where abuse was acknowledged to be a social construction, the term was used as if it was an entity amenable to the quantitative method of research. This deficit in the research had been highlighted by Wattam (1996) in her criticism of *Child Protection: Messages From Research* (DoH 1995). Examples of combining qualitative and quantitative research methods to study the processes of social interaction, based on everyday practice, are to be found in the work of Wattam (1992), Thorpe (1994), Buckley *et al.* (1997), Parton *et al.* (1997), Scott (1997) and Lawrence (2001). A particularly useful method of reviewing case records, referred to as 'document analysis', has revealed how social workers manage cases and also much about their decision-making processes.

It is now more generally recognized that the work of child protection is based on value judgements and therefore research into the subject, by its nature, cannot be value-free. As pointed out by Thorpe (1994: 29), 'It is a moral enterprise'. There remains the need to base services on empirical research and evaluation (Wattam 1992; Thorpe 1994; Vizard *et al.* 1995; Buckley *et al.* 1997; Scott 1997). How agencies present and evaluate their services and how they share information and communicate their respective roles in an accountable manner, are as important to families as they are to other agencies.

There is a need for more ethnographic research with regard to the processes involved in everyday practice. Until recently, much of child abuse research relied upon quantitative studies to establish parameters and the nature of the problem, relying on binary studies with no investigation into the human context. As the evolving social construction of child abuse becomes more apparent, the value of ethnographic studies is becoming more appreciated

Summary

The organizational and professional regulation of contemporary child protection systems is characterized by its emphasis on an interagency multidisciplinary approach. This system has developed in response to the management of child abuse as originally recommended by Henry Kempe and his associates in the 1960s. As the definitions of abuse broadened, and the number of professionals involved grew, it became apparent that there were many problems in its management. The Baglow multidimensional model was outlined as an example of the multidisciplinary method of working.

Although interagency and multidisciplinary management has been identified as the most effective method of working, it is recognized that many practice misunderstandings and conflicts can occur. Multidisciplinary conflicts were common in the past and these were often compounded by various professionals' frustrations at the difficulty of adequately protecting children from harm. In more recent times, there has been a backlash of parental rights groups and public opinion following various inquires into child abuse tragedies and this has exacerbated the difficulties of interagency cooperation and communication.

These difficulties can be grouped into two categories: surface problems and underlying theoretical issues. The first contains examples of practice-generated stresses for clients and staff, interagency conflicts, ambiguities and barriers to communication and cooperation. Actual practice examples have been included within the discussion of these difficulties. The second category refers to the little discussed paradox for social work professionals of having to make subjectivistic decisions while working in a positivistic framework. The multidisciplinary team is a combination of professions, some of whom operate within closed systems where objectivistic approaches are dominant. This method of working achieves its goals without regard to the specifics of individual morality. Social work is not such a closed system and views the individual *in situ*. Not only is there a need for a balance between these two systems but there is a more fundamental need to make this sometimes problematic relationship explicit. Further, this balance in the relationship needs to honoured by all of the professions in order for there to be an equality of status among interdisciplinary teams

The interagency multidisciplinary method of working will continue for the foreseeable future, but it is clear that there are a number of criticisms that need to be addressed. This chapter has identified and discussed five of these major criticisms, which include the need for a broadening of all of children's services to include in them a more subjectivist model. This would embrace the welfare of all children and not simply those who have been victims of abuse. The eligibility for services will need to broaden accordingly to become more than just a filtering system for the more obvious cases of abuse. These changes will only be achieved through societal, political and economic support. The chapter concluded by advocating a continuing quality assurance and evaluation programme for all children's services. Such a programme should supplement more general social research using both the positivistic and the subjectivist methods of inquiry.

5   Organizational perspectives of contemporary social work

Introduction

Social work takes place in an organizational context, so it is important that social workers understand the underlying principles and functions of organizations. A social work agency is a specific type of organization. It has been a long established tenet that the function of an agency will determine the scope and type of work to be accomplished. As discussed in the previous chapter, the restructuring of major child-focused organizations has been recommended in England, with the aim of incorporating social services, health and education into one department. In keeping with the tenet referred to above, social work will need to be redefined accordingly. Practitioners and managers will need to be equipped for this change and knowledge of organizational theory will help them to be better prepared to understand and contribute positively to the restructuring process.

The study of the development of organizational theory can be daunting and it would be outside the remit of this book to provide a full exposition of the various organizational theories. Rather, the aim here is to highlight the influence of those significant perspectives in social thought that have relevance to social work practice.

In this chapter some of the major organizational perspectives relating to social work are presented. There is currently a search for an organizational theory that will address the dynamic nature of society, the environment and recent technological developments. Various theories have been postulated and this chapter advocates the adoption of a specific version of *critical theory* as a dynamic basis for social work practice.

What is an organization?

Organizations are said to be the hallmark of modernity in that they are the representation of the division of labour associated with that period of social thought. Mullender and Perrott (1998) quote Robins (1990: 4), who defined an 'organization' as 'a consciously co-ordinated entity, with a relatively identifiable boundary, that functions on a relatively continuous basis to achieve a common goal or goals'. Organizations are part of complex societies and vary along a continuum of formality, from the formal bureaucratic organizations to the more informal and voluntary associations. Formal organizations are described as a large association of people, structured on impersonal lines and set up to achieve specific objectives (Giddens 1993). Child protection organizations are but one example of this. The study of organizations is said to be at the core of all social science (Perrow 1979).

Questions regarding how organinizations are formed, how they adapt to change and how individuals relate to an organization are of great interest to sociologists. The same questions have been asked of the specific organizational structures that underpin the basic concepts of child protection practice. Attempts to answer these questions have been made via various organizational theories.

There have been new and diverse perspectives on organizational theory over time, although none has been accepted uncritically (Clegg and Dunkerly 1980; Hasenfeld 1983; Hallett and Birchall 1992). Organizations are not insular phenomena, but exist in a dynamic relationship with each other. For example, the medical identification of child abuse, as developed by the research, changed the practice of child welfare organizations. These practices were subsequently superceded by legal, bureaucratic structures. Changes in any one of these organizations gave rise to change in the others. Additionally, social work, medical and legal organizations were all affected by the politics, culture and economics of the day. Organizational changes continue to take place as they adapt and respond to societal pressures. The proposed amalgamation of the major organizations of education, health and social services in the UK is one notable example of this process.

Organizational perspectives

Some of the main organizational perspectives that impinge upon child protection practice are described in the following sections.

The bureaucratic organization

Foremost among these perspectives is the 'ideal-type' bureaucracy (Weber 1946) whose administration pursues the rational achievement of organizational goals. This type of organization closely matches the rationalist-scientific perspective that was discussed previously. The basis of Weber's *rational model* is that organizations are distinguished by their reliance on authority and rules or procedures (Jones and May 1995). However, hierarchical and bureaucratized organizations are often criticized for being unwieldy and slow to function.

The bureaucratization of child protection work has emerged as a major disadvantage and the recognition of this fact set up new possibilities (Howe 1992). Howe quotes Dingwall *et al.* (1985: 28) to demonstrate that as child protection services have become more rationalized there have been more classifications of abuse, more procedures and more information to collect. The result has not been an improvement in services but, rather, alienated clients and produced practice-worn workers (Howe 1992; Marneffe 1996).

The human relations school perspective

The traditional Weberian, bureaucratic and rational theory of organization has been gradually adapted in successive phases to include the scientific management and the human relations perspectives. While scientific management theory focused on the needs and concerns of managers, emphasis was on the mechanistic, technical controls of production and the workforce itself (Giddens 1993). Policies were seen to be developed by experts and the practitioners' role was to implement them (Ife 1997). These policies were designed to improve industrial productivity in the early part of the twentieth century, without regard to the human impact. They were challenged in the mid-twentieth century by the *human relations school perspective*. This perspective was characterized by its emphasis on the morale of the workforce, leadership styles and group relationships. The proponents of the human relations perspective presented a model of organization that they claimed provided a balance of the goals of the organization with the needs of the workers (Jones and May 1995).

The systems perspective

The *systems perspective* of organizational theory emerged in the 1950s and 1960s and has been viewed by many writers as a necessary corrective to the rational perspective, as it places emphasis on the need to view organizations in the wider context of society in general (Etzioni 1964; Jones and May 1995: 43). Fundamental to the systems approach is its view of an organization as a network of subsystems, each being influenced by the behaviour of the others. The systems approach regards an organization as a living phenomenon and its relationship to the environment is therefore crucial to its survival. The organization is seen as having both internal and external needs that must be met to survive. Loyalty and commitment of the workers and funding are examples of internal and external needs respectively. This approach is said to provide a more holistic picture of an organization (Clegg and Dunkerly 1980).

A key aspect of this approach is the organization's relationship with the environment, and particularly with other organizations. For example, the processes whereby multidisciplinary services interact with families in child protection cases could be described in systemic terms (Minuchin and Fishman 1981; Mrazek 1981; Furniss 1983; Morrison 1990). This approach was helpful in so far as it summoned a structured response to help cope with the pressures associated with the management of referred cases. It also exposed the danger of having too narrow a knowledge base.

The systems perspective has been criticized on several counts. First, the elements of an organization are not always interdependent (Clegg and Dunkerly 1980). Second, organizations comprise individuals and it is they who react to the environment, often in unpredictable ways (Silverman 1970). Finally, the systems perspective has been criticized for not taking into account other factors such as the power relations inherent in family relationships (Smart 1989) and childcare service provision (O'Hagan and Dillenburger 1995). Despite its critics, this approach is useful in drawing attention to the internal and external needs of an organization and also in its raising of awareness in terms of the influences of other organistions on an organization's own functioning.

The feminist perspective

Feminist perspectives have clearly contributed to the contemporary under-standing of the authority dimension of human service organizations. It is of note that feminist perspectives do not simply analyse, but also suggest a political agenda for change (Dominelli and McLeod 1989). The systems approach in organizational theory had neglected the influence of patri-archy, and the feminist perspective pointed out that there has been an overall neglect of gender in organizational studies (Alvesson and Billing 1997), with gender being marginalized in organizational analysis (Martin 1994) and feminism being 'ghettoized' (Acker 1989). Alvesson and Billing (1997: 187) define ghettoization in this context as 'an intellectual domain that is isolated, self-contained, holds a socially subordinate, or low-status position, and is well demarcated'.

Feminist writers have argued that it is essential to understand gender relations in order to understand the roles of both workers and consumers

(Rowbotham 1989; McDowell and Pringle 1992). They have pointed to the dominant role that men play in managerial positions in human service organizations, particularly in government (Watson 1989). This is particularly relevant in the management of child sexual abuse, where the majority of social worker practitioners and their clients are women (Domenelli and McLeod 1989; O'Hagan and Dillenburger 1995). A feature of the feminist perspective is its focus on interpersonal relationships in organizations. This is a useful corrective to the detached and relatively impersonal stance adopted by the scientific management perspective and is in keeping with the more humanistic approach as advocated in this book.

The anti-racist perspective

The knowledge of an anti-racist perspective in the UK has added an extra dimension to our understanding of the suffering of ethnic minority children. As with feminism, anti-racism has revealed many deep-rooted stereotypes in society (Cooper 1993: 55).

Similarly, in Australia there has been acknowledgement that there is a need to take into account an anti-racist perspective in regard to the Aboriginal population. This was reflected in the *Royal Commission into Aboriginal Black Deaths in Custody* (Wyvill 1991). For many years in Australia there had been a neglect of and a failure to understand the needs of Aboriginal people. For instance, the operations of some governmental organizations, such as welfare services, are often at variance with the cultural values of Aboriginal people. Some assert that the very words 'social justice and rights' are a form of cultural dominance (Jones and May 1995: 71). These same authors have said that, 'in the Australian context it is vital to state that there is a distinctive Aboriginal view of organisations, and that social and welfare workers must be aware of this. This perspective is grounded in Aboriginal history, including the history of relations with non-Aboriginal people, and in particular the relations between Aboriginal people and state organisations' (pp. 68–9).

There is some evidence of attempts to incorporate the Aboriginal perspective, as outlined in the West Australian *Family and Children's Services 1997/98 Annual Report* (Family and Children's Services 1998). New outreach programmes for supporting Aboriginal families and communities are described in this document, together with a range of newly-funded services. Of special note is the fact that representation of Aboriginal people has been strengthened with the appointment of senior service staff across Western Australia. Similarly, the same need to understand and respond to ethnic minority groups applies to social workers in the UK. Discrimination must be considered in any discussion of organizational theory.

Contemporary social influences on child protection organization

The description and definition of various periods of time is referred to as the 'periodization of societies'. In sociological terms, the process refers to an intellectual attempt to describe discreet epochs in the past and to understand their relationship to contemporary society. This periodization of society depends largely on the manner in which society has been analysed. Various texts overlap descriptions of schools of thought and corresponding time frames for the various periodizations. This overlap and ambiguity is evident in contemporary debates concerning the differentiation between modernity and postmodernity.

As no firm boundaries exist between the competing discourses, the terms used in the periodization of social thought have had their critics. The definition of 'postmodernism' is no exception, as it is difficult to define due to its relativist stance and its resistance to objectivity (Turner 1992; Carter 1998). Despite these objections, various authors use the term 'postmodern' when commenting on the changing character of contemporary organizations (Jones and May 1995; Adams *et al.* 1998).

Changing patterns in society have led to the need for a reappraisal of organizational perspectives to enable a broader approach to child welfare (Parton *et al.* 1997; Parton 1998; Houston and Griffiths 2000). One suggestion is that services should abandon narrow screening practices that preclude many children and families who may benefit from social work assistance (Wattam 1996; King 1997; Parton 1998; Morris and Shepherd 2000). Over the years, resources have been channeled away from general welfare and into the identification of abusive families, and this is now being questioned (Parton 1991; Reder *et al.* 1993; Wattam 1996; Buckley *et al.* 1997; Parton *et al.* 1997). The theory informing these changes and the nomenclature ascribed to rapid societal change in general are situated in the current debates regarding the periodization of social thought.

The current period in time is often referred to as the 'postmodern period' and it is a time when radical changes are taking place in the organization of social work and child protection practice. The influence of postmodern thinking on child protection is well illustrated by the work of Howe (1994).

Postmodern influences on organizations involved in child protection

The pressures and criticisms that are faced by social workers in the child protection field are reflected in the four postmodern factors identified by

Howe. The major postmodern influences on human service organizations that he cites are 'pluralism, participation, power and performance' (1994: 523). He concludes that the culturally transcendent and transforming notions of progress and order that helped to form the child-centered and protectionist discourse are now being openly challenged. The modern influences that helped to create social work, defining the roles of worker and client, are now questioned. According to Howe, 'If being in a critical, self-reflexive, de-centred and deconstructive state of mind captures the mood of postmodernity, then social work, too, might be said to be in a postmodern mood' (p. 523).

Some authors have criticised Howe's categorization of postmodern influences, stating that his rejection of modernism is too sweeping and is ill-founded in relation to the nature of social work theory and practice (Smith and White 1997). Despite the criticism, other authors have supported Howe's view that some contemporary social work can be analysed in terms of postmodern influences (Parton 1994; Ife 1997; Parton *et al.* 1997; Parton and Marshall 1998). While some social work core values have remained the same (Biestek 1957) and have been the mainstay of practice for many, there have been recent challenges to these values in the form of the paradoxes inherent in the child protection discourse. The dilemmas and challenges facing the practitioner as identified by Howe (1994) are clearly evident in the workplace of today, whatever the preferred classification of society. The following examples from practice are given to illustrate the way Howe's four factors have influenced organizational perspectives.

Pluralism

The notion of *pluralism* and the tolerance of differences was a major impetus for the reorganization of family and children's services in Western Australia, based on the evaluative research of David Thorpe (1994). Nigel Parton, in the Foreword to *Evaluating Child Protection* (Thorpe 1994: x) refers to this reorganization as bringing about a desired shift in our attention, priorities and resources 'to child welfare work rather then child protection'.

The pluralist or postmodernist position allows for diversity and acknowledges class, region and culture (Ife 1997). Pluralism need not mean anarchy with total relativity and no structures (Clegg 1993). In recent times a more eclectic approach to organizational theory has developed, both in England and Australia, that attempts to combine structure and differentiation. For example, in 1998, Family and Children's Services in Western Australia held extensive consultation with that state's Council of Social Services and other interested bodies in the community with a view to their becoming part of the planning process to determine which services were to be funded (Family and Children's Services 1998). In order to succeed in the modern world, it seems that human services need to incorporate a humanistic perspective as well as other perspectives such as the feminist perspective and, in the Australian context, the Aboriginal perspective.

Participation

Participation is said to mean the acknowledgement and unconditional acceptance of all participants' rights and responsibilities, and this is most often cited as the strength of working in partnership with parents, as exemplified in the Children Act 1989 (Howe 1994). *Partnership in Child Protection: The Strategic Management Response* (Evans and Miller 1992) was a joint report between the National Institute for Social Work and the Office for Public Management, which upheld the right of representation of users and carers involved in child protection investigations. While upholding this right, Evans and Miller also concluded that it was not easily achieved. Relinquishing a traditional paternalistic stance in the name of partnership is an understandably uphill battle for child protection workers (Morrison 1996: 133).

Cases of public moral panic, exemplified by the way the press have pushed the rescue of children to the top of the agenda, are one of the major dilemmas for practitioners who are now expected to relinquish their traditional roles. This has generated a fear of failure among practitioners and the cost of legal representation for parents is also a key inhibitor in this process of participation.

National parent support groups such as Parents Against Injustice and the Family Rights Group (1991) have helped to redefine the essence of working in partnership with families (Amphlett 1992; Cooper 1993). However, due to financial crisis the demise of Parents Against Injustice was recently reported (Brindle 1999). As a result of the Cleveland, Rochdale and Orkney child sexual abuse investigations, partnership with parents during the last two decades has been undermined and the image of the child protection worker has also suffered (Cooper 1993: 78).

Documents such as the *Declaration of the Rights of the Child* (United Nations 1989) stress the rights of children to engage also in the process of participation. Although the Children Act 1989 legislated that children's feelings and wishes should be ascertained, there is no requirement proposed in this Act for consulting children (Jeffries *et al.* 1997). In a study into divorce proceedings, Jeffries *et al.* found that children could articulate their wishes sensitively, although in fact no particular weight was given by the courts to their views. For empowerment of parents and children to be realized, more legal support is required. Empowerment in this context is defined as the goal of enabling individuals or groups to express their own needs and rights and, as such, incorporates both a personal and political process. It can be appreciated that the concept of participation remains an active challenge to contemporary practice.

Power

Howe's third nominated postmodern influence is *power* and has been alluded to in the previous examples as being central to the structures and processes of organizations. Jones and May (1995) believe that there is considerable theoretical debate about the meaning of power as distinguished from influence and authority. They conclude that power is the capacity of an organization to force compliance and, equally important, the ability of an organization to resist any demand made on it *for* compliance.

Two examples from child welfare practice illustrate this capacity for the use of power. First, in Western Australia, the health authorities were of the opinion that the health needs of specific groups, such as infants born in country areas, were being adequately met. This opinion was promulgated despite the views of the local population and the professionals working in the area who deemed otherwise. The same health authorities conducted epidemiological surveys in order to reassert that these health needs were being met. However, the results of the surveys showed otherwise. The health authorities felt bound to take action in the light of the survey results but were not previously prepared to take this action merely on the basis of reports from other sources.

Second, a family wrongly accused of abuse of their child were unable to ask for reparation from the protection agency that made the assessment (Amphlett 1992). The family were inhibited from doing so out of fear that the agency would label them as uncooperative and place them in a more vulnerable position. Howe (1994) has said that by classifying clients and assembling concerns, social workers play a key role in the regulation of society's marginal members.

It has been said that the professionals who generally frame the questions are those who already have the answers; that is, they speak from positions of power (Dingwall *et al.* 1983; Wattam 1992; Cooper 1993, Howe 1994; Ife 1997). Cleaver and Freeman (1995) reported in their investigation of the child protection process that the families concerned had adopted different perspectives from the professionals. The families' perspective was one of fear, anxiety and the need to cope. The professionals on the other hand needed to adopt a stance to avoid blame and adhere to procedure. All of the parties concerned experienced stress. Similar findings were reported by Baglow (1990) in his identification of stressful activities for both families and professionals.

In a survey of parental responses to their referral to statutory bodies, following the identification of non-accidental injury of their child, the need to offer more emotional support to parents was identified (Lawrence and Harrison 1994). One of the major messages from this evaluative study was a plea from the parents for the professionals to *listen to their stories*. Professionals may be seen to withdraw personally from such encounters under the guise of adopting a so-called objectivist stance, in an attempt to protect themselves from conflict.

The subjective existence of those involved is sometimes greatly over-looked by professionals seeking to protect themselves in this situation and avoid personal blame. This is similar to Parton *et al*.'s (1997) findings that social workers tend to operate in 'risk insurance'. It would seem more appropriate to aim for a congruence of perspectives between all participants, with the professionals adopting a more subjectivist approach. Cleaver and Freeman (1995) identified that where there was a greater amount of congruence, outcomes were considered to be better for all concerned.

The aforementioned recurrent scenario illustrates how the traditional collating of risk factors can be replaced by an acceptance of the family that allows a deconstruction of child abuse assessment. A desire to achieve congruence between the practitioner and the family would encourage all those involved to express their points of view, experience and concerns. This would also include the narrative of the child, where possible. Deconstruction of child abuse in this sense is basic to its assessment, in that it looks for the subjective meaning behind the information presented in a referral. In this way, the uniqueness of individuals is respected and the 'meaning' of each family's life assists in the assessment. A practitioner would generally bring to an assessment a prior body of knowledge of the supposed causes of child abuse, together with information on the individual family concerned. Congruity would be achieved by supplementing this knowledge with the narrative of the family. This implies the necessity of the practitioner adopting a phenomenological, accepting, genuine, empathetic and non-judgmental approach. Once again, this would indicate a return to the core values of the social work profession, with its emphasis on the central importance of promoting the essential qualities of a therapeutic relationship, as identified in the work of Rogers (1951) and Biestek (1957).

The deconstruction of child abuse is necessary to empower families, as it does not assume that there is one right answer for any situation. The deconstruction of abuse promotes anti-oppressive practice and would allow for differences of perspective, to be discussed within a reflexive framework in which the child and all the participants are heard.

Achieving the goal of empowerment requires interpersonal communication skills in working with marginalized groups, as well as a commitment to the establishment of sympathetic organizational and political structures. It is ironic that those who generally espouse equality are frequently, if indirectly, perpetuating inequality. What appears to be contradictory and dichoto-mous can be turned to an advantage when located and managed success-fully. Ife (1997: 42) has demonstrated that the hierarchic/anarchist view can also be described in the organizational terms of a 'top-down, bottom-up' dichotomy. Accountability to consumers and to society can be seen to be more important (bottom-up approach) than accountability to management, although successful empowerment of consumers will inevitably encompass a combination of both. Ife refers to the work of the Brotherhood of St Laurence as an example of the model of service users and management working together. This organization is managed by the community themselves (Ife 1997: 44, 149). The corollary to this is that human service organizations need to conduct a critical analysis of their ability to know and respond to their consumers. They should also be prepared to accept that the results of such an analysis might not be in accord with the established practice of the organization. In the case of child protection services, management might institute complaint procedures to help clients who may feel aggrieved following an investigation. However, the outcome of the complaint may not always result in direct change of procedure for various reasons – for example, a lack of resources allocated to such reparation. However, where consumer evaluation surveys are conducted routinely and taken seriously, the opinions of clients are more likely to be taken into consideration and appropriate action taken (Lawrence and Harrison 1994).

Performance

Finally, the fourth postmodern factor described by Howe (1994: 527) is, *performance*. Howe recounts the fact that 'modernity' has rejected the 'premodern', divine law, social order with its connotations of absolute authority. The locus of control in thought has shifted from a sacred order to the secular state management of society. Scientific strategies for rigorous analysis of human organizations have developed in an effort to enhance reliability and predictability. An individual's social performance has tended to be commodified, viewed and measured in terms of output. For Howe, organizational work in postmodernity can no longer simply claim to be achieving what it set out to do; it needs to be able to demonstrate such claims.

With organizational emphasis on contractual agreements, service provisions and social rights, we see that 'clients and their behaviour are defined in legal and, increasingly, in economic, service and consumer terms' (Howe 1994: 528). This led to social work practice itself being revised in terms of the 'scientific management' of organization (Jones and May 1995: 39). Jones and May have stressed the significance of Weber's emphasis on the importance of this 'legal-rational authority' as being a basic characteristic of almost all organizations.

The bureaucratisation of social work was characterized by the inundation of policies and procedures for recommended child protection practice after each child abuse inquiry in Britain (Howe 1992). Thereafter, the discourse of managerialism emerged with its accompanying stress on accountability that contributed to the commodification of social work practice. In Australian public administration literature, commitment to the processes of accountability, performance appraisal, programme evaluation, consumer audits, outcome standards and other quality assurance measures has also been referred to as 'managerialism' (Jones and May 1995; Ife 1997). While an unqualified mechanistic view of any new scientific organizational process can be criticized as strictly top-down and dehumanizing, for some purposes, when coupled with other market forces and professional ideals, it may become a source of positive change (Ife 1997; Mullender and Perrott 1998). An example of such a positive change was previously discussed in reference to the consumer survey conducted with parents as part of an established quality assurance programme at a children's hospital. The results of this study highlighted the desirability of developing a model of management that recognized the need to offer more emotional support and better information to parents, allowing their point of view to be heard and respected (Lawrence and Harrison 1994). Thereafter, the children's hospital reorganized its model of intervention accordingly.

During the last two decades, it has become an accepted strategy of scientific management to obtain information from consumers and workers alike as to the effectiveness of the work of their agency (Howe 1994; Ife 1997). The trend towards analysing the effectiveness of an agency has seen the development of various methods and strategies. Jones and May (1995) developed a framework for analysing and evaluating the actual and potential power, authority and influence of consumers in an organization. These same authors recommended strategies to improve organization-consumer relations across the human services.

The assessment of performance was seen by some as a postmodern attempt to commodify action. It was said that the focus of social work was no longer on the actor, but on the action, and thus task-oriented (Howe 1994). Jones and May (1995: 399) make an important observation when they refer to the need to transcend managerialism by developing a broader perspective that reflects a concern for social justice, excellence and expansion of organizational goals to meet the ever-growing number of welfare demands faced by society. This viewpoint is worthy of emphasis as it reflects the incorporation of the social work professional code of ethics.

It is clear from the foregoing account that there have been many forces impinging on the myriad of human service organizational perspectives. The four contemporary perspectives discussed above are examples of this. It would appear that organizational viewpoints have developed not by earlier stances being superseded by newer perspectives, but rather by their addition to existing forms. This suggests that this whole network of perspectives must be considered in order to understand the behaviour of the individuals and the environmental characteristics that constitute human service organizations. The challenge for social work is to combine and reflexively integrate the various complex principles of organization into a contemporary theory of social work.

Critical perspectives for social work

It is clear that the various organizational perspectives all have something to contribute to the theoretical base for multidisciplinary management of child abuse. The challenge for child protection is to integrate the relevant aspects of these perspectives. As child protection work occurs within human service organizations, encompassing specific knowledge, skills and values, it should be informed by a commitment to social justice, an awareness of gender and racial differences, and a belief in human rights. However, human service organizations differ in terms of values and patterns of communication, as well as in management styles. Each may also align to a different theoretical perspective. It would hardly be surprising, therefore, in such a complex field, to discover that the search for an all-embracing theory of organization continues to be elusive. Some elements from all of the perspectives discussed above need to be reflexively brought to bear on the challenges of contemporary practice. Two of the most influential perspectives for child protection practice are discussed in the following sections.

The ecological model

In an attempt to draw together the positive contributions of previous organizational theories, an 'ecological' model was suggested by Cooper (1993) and David (1994). Cooper's model is a dynamic one in that it addresses the reciprocal interaction of individuals within the larger context of the cultural, political and legal influences of society. The importance of the ecological model in child protection, according to David (1994: 7) 'is the way in which child abuse and attitudes towards children will be seen as dependent upon the overarching ideology, as well as the political and economic climate, of a society or subculture, not simply as emanating from one person, family or community groups'. Cooper favours this model in his attempt to develop greater understanding and a knowledge base for action with regard to children.

In ecological theory, organizations are considered to survive or otherwise in a manner analogous to animal and plant life, thriving on or adapting to environmental changes. This is particularly relevant at the present time of economic constraint, when social services need to compete for funding. The ecological model shares common themes with systems theory as it attempts to describe the interrelatedness of actor and environment, thus highlighting the need for a more subjectivist approach in child protection.

A version of critical theory for social work

The search for an all-embracing organizational perspective for interagency practice in the field of social work and child protection has led to a number of social theorists contributing to the development of 'critical theory'. Critical theory is a complex area of social theorizing, named and developed by the Frankfurt Institute which had been set up at Frankfurt University in 1923 (Pusey 1995; Calhoun 1995).

One version of the many varieties of critical theory of particular relevance to social work practice is advocated by Ife (1997). He refers to the following authors in support of this: Geuss (1981), Ray (1993), Morrow and Brown (1994), Calhoun (1995) and Dryzek (1995). This approach recommends not choosing between the different 'critical' theories and perspectives, but rather developing an integrated approach from a range of perspectives on organizational analysis.

The critical perspective recognizes that an interpretative understanding and the ability to communicate are not sufficient for a human services organization to function properly. Of signigicance is also the need to incorporate a broader based analysis of a situation. Both these perspectives would be necessary in the formation of an integrated approach. This critical theory is based in the humanist tradition and is not concerned with either personal or political aspects alone, but with *both*. It is in this sense that this approach is compatible with feminist perspectives and their emphasis on the personal as political (Ife 1997: 134). This perspective also recognizes the mutual empowerment of individuals and groups.

The process of self-reflection that is contained within this critical perspective is utilized, not only to help an individual subject struggling against the internalization of a dominant ideology, but also to help a group to develop reflexive knowledge of the political forces of the day. Thus, it becomes the goal to develop reflexive knowledge to achieve emancipation from self-imposed constraints (Leonard 1997). In this way, it can be seen that the 'critical' perspective lies within the humanist tradition with its goal being the liberation of the individual. As such, this version of critical theory has a defence against dogma and would recognize the frailty of the concept of the expert. In addition, as a critical discourse, it contains an openness to communication with politically significant others (Leonard 1997).

This version of critical theory recognizes that working with individuals has a political aspect and in child protection this involves working together with people who often have competing and conflicting interests. It also recognizes the need for social workers to reflexively consider their own personal position in an organization, the power or authority of their organization as well as the need to analyse the political environment of consumers. This critical perspective is further discribed as follows: 'The capacity to link the personal and the political, the capacity to develop community-based structures, the insistence that the interests of the most vulnerable and disadvantaged be included in any alternative development and that their voices be heard, the commitment to social justice and human rights, and the capacity to practice at both an individual and a community level' (Ife 1997: 206).

This approach to the theory of organizations suggests an integration of perspectives to form a particular version of critical theory. For the practitioner this would mean not only being trained in the interpersonal skills employed in casework, but also being educated in the economic and political contexts of the day.

Summary

This chapter has argued that social workers need to have a knowledge base and a clear, critical understanding of organizational perspectives. It commenced by defining an organization. This was followed by a discussion of various classical organizational models that have contributed to the structure and practice of child protection and child welfare work.

Max Weber's classical exposition of bureaucracy was described as the model that underpins modern formal organizations. The bureaucratic model and other traditional perspectives have needed modification to accommodate the ever-increasing complexity of contemporary societal issues, each a demanding positive response. Today, bureaucracies coexist within a plethora of newer perspectives. Scientific management, systems theory, feminism, anti-racist theory, ecological theory and, in Australia, Aboriginal perspectives are all seen to have specific contributions to make to a dynamic and integrated theory of organizational practice. These perspectives were reviewed in order to place the service provision of the multidisciplinary interagency method of operation in the context of a theory for contemporary social work.

An overview of the sociological process of periodization was presented. Epochs from history to present-day society have been identified by sociologists and these periods receive a nomenclature that has no fixed or definite boundaries. Debates about such categorizations are numerous and this is most evident in current divisions of thought with reference to modern and postmodern periodization. Despite the debates, many writers would agree that changes in social work practice may be best described through reference to the growth of postmodern influences. Four of these were described.

In keeping with postmodernism, no one theory or perspective is sufficient for a full understanding of any particular human service organization, let alone interagency working. For this reason, an appreciation of the various perspectives is important to be able to synthesize the most appropriate elements for any particular need. This integration of the micro and the macro aspects of social work practice was recognized in the discussion of critical theory. The integration of the personal and the political perspectives may represent the most useful framework for the management of child abuse. The challenge of contemporary practice requires the development of a critical model of service delivery to draw together and symbolize the dynamic forces that exist in society today.

6 Implications for the future

Introduction

This chapter makes recommendations for future services. It also discusses existing current governmental initiatives in England and Western Australia for children's welfare. Recommendations are made for improved services in the light of the analysis of the major issues as outlined in the previous chapters.

A broader welfare perspective for children and families

Debate has been introduced in the child protection discourse concerning the need to reconceptualize child protection practice within a broader welfare perspective (Thorpe 1994; Parton 1998: Houston and Griffiths 2000; Spratt *et al*. 2000). The broader perspective suggested by these authors is reflected in the Green Paper *Every Child Matters* (DfES 2003). This initiative is currently being implemented through the establishment of children's trusts, bringing together local health, education and social services.

At the time of going to press this initiative remains in pilot form in 35 local authorities. Plans for expansion of the programme to include all local authorities in England are proposed for 2006. The Children Bill, which was presented to the House of Lords in July 2004, gives effect to the legislative proposals set out in the Green Paper. In addition the Government published *Every Child Matters: Next Steps* which provides an overview of the legislation and how the proposals might work in practice. In Western Australia, the Child Welfare Amendment Act 2002 has placed the rights of the child as paramount in respect of welfare issues. In addition, new inter-agency coordination and collaborative initiatives to promote family welfare and children's best interests have been implemented by the Family and Children's Services. These programme initiatives have been introduced in an attempt to broaden the department's focus to include a more welfare-based perspective to offer universal services to all children in need.

However, despite these current efforts to broaden child welfare services in England and Australia there continues to be a primary focus on child protection and the assessment of risk. In these areas the child protection residual model continues to dominate. In this model resources are focused on the identification of abuse and assessment of risk and there is a consequent neglect of other children in need.

Past efforts to overcome problems in the child protection service were couched in a continuing positivistic framework. This led to a proliferation of guidelines recommended by official inquiries and governmental reports, but without any consequent improvement in the accurate assessment of risk. The inability of this increased bureaucracy to solve the problems, together with the ever-increasing number of referrals, have been additional factors in the need for a reappraisal of the present method of service delivery.

If a broader perspective were to be adopted for child welfare services there would be direct implications for training of practitioners and their managers. Any suggested change in policy direction would need to locate the practitioner in the process. Practitioners would need to be helped to understand the value of working within a more reflexive and subjectivist model.

The need for a broader perspective of welfare for children and families to include a more generalist approach is supported by the literature (Lawrence 2001). There is evidence of a correlation between incidences of child abuse and socioeconomic circumstances. The traditional view that focuses on the psychopathology of the individual may need to change to take into account the stresses created by adverse socioeconomic factors as likely causes of child abuse. The nature of the positivistic framework in the assessment of child abuse denies any negative environmental circumstances with its emphasis on the acquisition of forensic evidence when there may be more pressing socioeconomic needs to be addressed. A more generalist welfare approach would be more likely to result in the identification of the *total* needs of the family. Moreover, the positivistic approach tends to inhibit the development of a therapeutic relationship.

The adoption of a subjectivist and more reflexive approach would be possible in a generalist welfare system, as described in the following recommendation.

The preventative approach to child welfare services

Under the present method of operation, child protection practitioners generally become involved in the family only when there is a crisis referral. A preventative policy towards child welfare would involve practitioners in a more proactive role. Ideally, the practitioner would provide a primary service and become more involved in parent education, parent support and family empowerment. It appears from current research (Lawrence 2001) that practitioners feel the need to humanize contacts, whether with colleagues from other agencies or with clients. This would give support to the view that practitioners would welcome a more proactive role.

A preventative approach is a supportive one and so would operate without the stigma some families now feel through having to ask for help once a crisis stage has been reached. The aim would be to establish a support service that would be accepted as an institution in society to which families would go as a matter of routine. Such an institution would be locally based and cover a wide range of services addressing the needs of all families and not just those considered to be 'failing'. Attendance would be voluntary and encouraged through appropriate advertizing and possibly operated via interagency cooperation with other services involved with child welfare. Such work would necessitate the need to adopt a reflexive role that does not narrowly view the family within a punitive perspective. This would involve a complete reordering of priorities and a reallocation of resources.

More reflexive practice

The concept of reflexivity in practice has been referred to as the circular process by which our thoughts affect our actions, which in turn affect the situation with which we are dealing (Payne 1998). This approach would offer feedback through the reactions of others involved, which can affect how we understand and think about a situation. This implies a circularity of function and can be related to the role of empathetic listening in the therapeutic relationship – that is, the holding of a mirror to clients in order to reflect their feelings and ideas back to them and then to reflect on this understanding together. The intention is to better achieve the congruence and empathy that is the essence of a helping relationship. This is the opposite of the more rigid, authoritarian approach born of an objectivist model within which the practitioner is perceived as the expert.

The concept of partnership with parents, as advocated in the child protection discourse, would be reflected in this greater mutuality between practitioner and client. It is not unreasonable to suggest that the rejection of the expert and the adoption of a more phenomenological approach to the relationship, as well as the acknowledgement of situated judgements, would increase the reliability of assessments and ultimately be of benefit to all concerned.

This viewpoint receives particular support from the feminist movement which has criticized the scientific-objective standpoint on the grounds of gender bias (Smart and Sevenhuijsen 1989). Parton *et al.* (1997) and Parton (1998) would also support a move away from the role of the expert. Parton *et al.* (1997) consider that the positivistic model decontextualizes children and families, thus inhibiting the establishment of therapeutic relationships.

Traditionally, the social work profession has emphasized the relationship with the individual *in situ*. A major challenge for child protection practitioners is the ability to retain a humanistic perspective while recognizing the need to incorporate legal mandates in day-to-day practice.

It is timely for a refocusing of children's services to include the situated judgement necessary when attempting to make objective decisions (Thorpe 1994; Parton *et al.* 1997; Parton 1998; Houston and Griffiths 2000; Morris and Shepherd 2000). A similar situation can be seen to exist in psychology. A practising psychologist would retain objectivity through psychometric testing, but would form conclusions on an individual case by supplementing the test results with subjective clinical judgements. The latter would probably include a phenomenological approach to obtain the client's perceptions. According to Houston and Griffiths (2000), a move towards a more subjectivist approach would allow contemporary practice to offer services that are considered to be more appropriate and meaningful to the needs of children and families.

A major paradox for the child protection system is related to the doubts now cast upon the 'scientific' assessment procedure. As feminists had been emphasizing, it is impossible to intervene in a reliably 'scientific' way. Yet to date it has not been acceptable to admit this, as many in wider society would not understand the harm to morale for both practitioner and society (King 1997). The need to acknowledge that some decisions were morally based seemed to indicate that a more reflexive approach to assessment is needed. A balance of perspectives is now required in such complex circumstances that ultimately call for a legal and moral judgement to be made.

A Commissioner for Children and a Minister for Children

While some changes for future child welfare services might be a matter of internal reorganization and commitment to a new method of working, their introduction would also require political support to achieve the transitions. This is a matter over which social workers do not have direct control. Although there has been tacit agreement by successive governments in England to promote the welfare of children as reflected in numerous reports and Acts of Parliament, it is only very recently that a Minister for Children has been appointed.

The plan to appoint a Commissioner for Children and Young People in England, as proposed in the Children Bill and as already in place in Wales, Northern Ireland and Scotland, is to be welcomed as at last children will be given a vehicle through which to express their opinions and needs. While the appointment of a Minister for Children is to be applauded, a Commissioner's role would be able to promote children's rights and well-being independent of political influences. The Commissioner would also need to have direct links to the Minister for Children in order to ensure statutory backing for programmes and adequate resources.

In Western Australia, a new Directorate for Children and Young People has recently been created. While the creation of this new office is laudable it remains part of the Family and Children's Services and has not yet gained the prominence that would be achieved if it were a department in its own right. Although there is a ministerial department for children and families, as yet there is no Minister for Children in Western Australia who would be able to influence government policy directly. The Gordon Inquiry (Gordon 2002) made a recommendation for a Commissioner for Children in Western Australia, although this has yet to be realized.

The value of an appointment of an independent Commissioner for Children and a Minister for Children cannot be overestimated. The Minister for Children in England at present has a wide brief containing educational services, children's social services and health. However, there are often gaps in services for children with specific disadvantages who may have no official voice with which to make their dissatisfaction heard. The lack of consultation with children applies in numerous situations globally, whether in the workplace, education or the planning of leisure pursuits. It is only recently that attempts have been made to listen to children's opinions in custody disputes and foster placements, although the manner in which this is done is open to criticism as children can easily feel intimidated. Establishment of an independent Commissioner for Children would help to ensure that the child's voice is heard.

7　Conclusions

The evolving social constructions of child abuse and childhood have led to a burgeoning of definitions of abuse, possible perpetrators and ambiguities as to the nature of childhood. This in turn has led to an increasing number of referrals, problems of service delivery and the questioning of the system's efficiency. There is some evidence that only a minority of those cases investigated reach prosecution (Wattam 1992) although much time and many resources are devoted to the investigation of cases of possible child abuse. Too many cases continue to be seen unnecessarily under the child protection umbrella when their needs might be better met by improved family support provision. The challenge to the residual model of child protection, with its emphasis on the identification of individual psychopathology in cases of child abuse, continues to be a matter of debate.

The value of adopting a multidisciplinary approach for the management of child abuse, with cooperation between agencies involved in children's health and welfare, is recognized in both the literature and in practice. This approach has developed in accordance with recommended policy ideals and comprehensive, well-resourced systems of operation. Despite these positive developments, there have been expressions of concern that some challenges remain and that a number of surface as well as underlying dilemmas still need to be addressed. These problems and dilemmas are concerned with both practical and theoretical issues.

Questions have arisen about the governmentally sanctioned machinery of combined agencies which sift through referred allegations of child abuse, dealing with some and rejecting others. Various attempts are being made in England to rationalize these procedures to encompass all children in need, with broader-based welfare services of a supportive and preventative nature. While this is to be applauded, many underlying challenges remain that will require a change of focus for professional social work practice. This will have direct implications for in-service training for current employees as well as for those undergoing initial training.

The practical and theoretical environment in which the work of child protection takes place, together with challenges to this professional activity, have been outlined in this book. As these challenges are faced, changes will be required, not only in child protection practice, but also in central government policy. The rights of children and families need to be acknowledged at all levels of society and especially supported by governmental initiatives.

The profession of social work has traditionally been defined by its helping role in society. Practitioners have worked to identify and help rectify societal deficits in order to enhance the lives of individuals and communities. In some areas of child protection practice, societal challenges to redefine and limit this role have had to be overcome. Despite these negative influences, many social work professionals have remained dedicated to the service of children and families.

Currently, there are increasing opportunities for social workers to redefine their roles and articulate anew the unique skills of their profession in working with children and family services. The distinctive contribution of establishing a therapeutic helping relationship with children and families needs to be articulated by the profession. Above all, there is a need for society to more readily accept the value of social work as a positive and essential helping profession. It is clearly up to the profession to express this message.

References

ACCCA (Advisory and Coordinating Committee on Child Abuse) (1986) *Child Abuse: Strategies for Prevention and Protection Conference,* Perth, Western Australia.

ACCCA (Advisory and Coordinating Committee on Child Abuse) (1989) *Report on Child Abuse and Neglect Statistics.* Perth: ACCCA.

ACCCA (Advisory and Coordinating Committee on Child Abuse) (1992) *Report on Child Abuse and Neglect Statistics.* Perth: ACCCA.

Acker, J. (1989) *Making Gender Visible in Feminism and Sociological Theory.* Newbury Park, CA: Sage.

Adams, R., Dominelli, L. and Payne, M. (eds) (1998) *Social Work: Themes, Issues and Debates.* London: Macmillan.

Adler, R. (1996) Twenty years on, time to take stock, *Child Abuse and Neglect,* 20(6): 473–6.

Alaszewski, A. and Harrison, L. (1988) Literature review: collaboration between welfare agencies, *British Journal of Social Work,* 18(6): 635–47.

Alvesson, M. and Billing, Y. (1997) *Understanding Gender and Organizations.* London: Sage.

Amphlett, S. (1992) System abuse and gatekeeping. *Paper in Partnership in Child Protection, The Strategic Management Response.* London: National Institute for Social Work.

Anthony, G., Jenkins, J., Thompson, K. and Watkeys, J. (1988) Child sexual abuse: interagency collaboration in diagnosis, investigation and management within South Glamorgan, *Public Health,* 102: 237–44.

Archard, D. (1993) *Children: Rights and Childhood.* London: Routledge.

Archard, D. (1999) Can child abuse be defined? in M. King (ed.) *Moral Agendas for Children's Welfare,* pp. 74–89. London: Routledge.

Ariès, P. (1962) *Centuries of Childhood.* Harmondsworth: Penguin.

Armstrong, D. (1979) How to avoid burnout, *Child Abuse and Neglect,* 3: 145–9.

Ashley, D. (1992) Habermas and the completion of 'The Project of Modernity', in B. Turner (ed.) *Theories of Modernity and Postmodernity,* pp. 88–107. London: Sage.

Baglow, L. (1990) A multidimensional model for the treatment of child abuse: a framework for cooperation, *Child Abuse and Neglect*, 14: 387–95.

Bandura, A. (1986) *Social Foundations of Thought and Action*. Englewood Cliffs, NJ: Prentice Hall.

Beck, U. (1992) *Risk Society*. London: Sage.

Beck, U., Giddens, A. and Lash, S. (1994) *Reflexive Modernization*. Cambridge: Polity Press.

Becker, H. and Barnes, H.E. (eds) (1961) *Social Thought from Lore to Science*, 3rd edn. New York: Dover.

Bell, D. (1976) *The Cultural Contradictions of Capitalism*. New York: Basic Books.

Bell, S. (1988) *When Salem Came to the Boro*. London: Pan.

Best, J. (ed.) (1989) *Images of Issues Typifying Contemporary Social Problems*. New York: Aldine de Gruyter.

Biestek, F. (1957) *The Casework Relationship*. London: Unwin University Books.

Birchall, E. (1989) The frequency of child abuse – what do we really know? in O. Stevenson (ed.) *Child Abuse: Profession Practice and Public Policy*. Hemel Hempstead: Wheatsheaf.

Birchall, E. with Hallett, C. (1995) *Working Together in Child Protection*. London: HMSO.

Blagg, H. (1989) Fighting the stereotypes – 'ideal' victims in the inquiry press, in H. Blagg, J. Hughes and C. Wattam (eds) *Child Sexual Abuse: Listening, Hearing and Validating the Experiences of Children*. Harlow: Longman.

Blagg, H. and Stubbs, P. (1988) A child centred practice? Multiagency approaches to child sexual abuse, *Practice*, 2(1): 12–19.

Boss, P. (1980) *On the Side of the Child: An Australian Perspective on Child Abuse*. Melbourne: Fontana/Collins.

Bourdieu, P. (1993) *Sociology in Question*. London: Sage.

Bowlby, J. (1951) *Child Care and the Growth of Love*. Harmondsworth: Penguin.

Bowlby, J. (1969) *Attachment*. Harmondsworth: Penguin.

Boyden, J. (1990) Childhood and the policymakers: a comparative perspective on the globalization of childhood, in A. James and A. Prout (eds) *Constructing and Reconstructing Childhood*, pp. 184–215. London: Falmer.

Brindle, D. (1999) Painful departure, *Guardian*, 14 April: 6–7.

British Psychological Society (2003) *Child Protection – Safeguarding Children and Young People From Abuse, Harm and Neglect: The Responsibilities of Chartered Psychologists*. Leicester: British Psychological Society.

Buckingham, D. (2000) *After the Death of Childhood: Growing Up in the Age of Electronic Media*. Oxford: Blackwell Priory.

Buckley, H., Skehill, C. and O'Sullivan, E. (1997) *Child Protection Practices in Ireland: A Case Study*. Dublin: Oak Tree Press.

Burr, V. (1995) *An Introduction to Social Constructionism*. London: Routledge.

Butler-Sloss, Lord Justice E. (1988) *Report of the Inquiry into Child Abuse in Cleveland 1987*, CM 412. London: HMSO.

Calhoun, C. (1995) *Critical Social Theory*. Oxford: Blackwell.

Campbell, B. (1988) *Unofficial Secrets*. London: Virago.

Carmody, M. (1990) Midnight companions: social work involvement in the development of sexual assault services in New South Wales, *Australian Social Work*, 43(4): 9–16.

Carter, J. (ed.) (1998) *Postmodernity and the Fragmentation of Welfare*. New York: Routledge.

Challis, L., Fuller, S., Henwood, M., Klein, R., Plowden, W., Webb, A., Whittingham, P. and Wistow, C. (1988) *Joint Approaches to Social Policy – Rationality and Practice*. Cambridge: Cambridge University Press.

Cleaver, H. and Freeman, M. (1995) *Parental Perspectives in Cases of Suspected Child Abuse*. London: HMSO.

Clegg, S.R. (1993) *Modern Organizations*. London: Sage.

Clegg, S.R. and Dunkerly, D. (1980) *Organization, Class and Control*. London: Routledge & Kegan Paul.

Conte, J.R. (1984) Progress in treating the sexual abuse of children, *Social Work*, 9(May/June): 263–86.

Conway, M. (ed.) (1997) *Recovered Memories and False Memories*. Oxford: Oxford University Press.

Cooley, C.H. (1912) *Human Nature and the Social Order*. New York: Scribners.

Cooper, D.M. (1993) *Child Abuse Revisited: Children, Society and Social Work*. Buckingham: Open University Press.

Cooper, D.M. and Ball, D. (1987) *Social Work and Child Abuse*. London: Macmillan.

Corby, B. (2000) *Child Abuse: Towards a Knowledge Base*, 2nd edn. Buckingham: Open University Press.

Courtois, C. (1997) Delayed memories of child sexual abuse: critique of the controversy and clinical guidelines, in M. Conway (ed.) *Recovered Memories and False Memories*, pp. 206–29. Oxford: Oxford University Press.

Cunningham, H. (1991) *The Children of the Poor: Representations of Childhood Since the Seventeenth Century*. Oxford: Blackwell.

Dale, P. and Davies, M. (1985) A model of intervention in child abusing families: a wider systems view, *Child Abuse and Neglect*, 9: 449–55.

David, T. (ed.) (1994) *Protecting Children from Abuse: Multiprofessionalism and the Children Act*. London: Trentham Books.

Davies, M. (1995) *Childhood Sexual Abuse and the Construction of Identity*. London: Taylor & Francis.

De Mause, L. (ed.) (1974) *The History of Childhood: The Evolution of Parent– Child Relationships as a Factor in History*. Leicester: The Psychological Press.

Denzin, N.K. (1977) *Childhood Socialization*. San Francisco: Jossey-Bass.

Derrida, J. (1976) *Of Grammatology*. Baltimore, MD: Johns Hopkins University Press.

Derrida, J. (1978) *Writing and Difference*. Chicago: University of Chicago Press.

DfES (Department for Education and Skills) (2003) *Every Child Matters*. London: The Stationery Office.

DfES (Department for Education and Skills) (2004) *Every Child Matters: Next Steps*. London: The Stationery Office.

DHSS (Department of Health and Social Security (1973) *A Report from the Working Party on the Collaboration between the NHS and Local Government on its Activities to the End of 1972*. London: HMSO.

DHSS (Department of Health and Social Security (1986) *Child Abuse: Working Together. A Draft Guide for Inter-agency Co-operation for the Protection of Children*. London: HMSO.

DHSS (Department of Health and Social Security (1988) *Diagnosis of Child Sexual Abuse: Guidance for Doctors*. London: HMSO.

Dingwall, R. (1989) Some problems about predicting child abuse and neglect, in O. Stevenson (ed.) *Child Abuse: Public Policy and Professional Practice*. Hemel Hempstead: Harvester Wheatsheaf.

Dingwall, R., Eekelaar, J. and Murray, T. (1983) *The Protection of Children: State Intervention and Family Life*. Oxford: Blackwell.

DoH (Department of Health) (1991a) *Child Abuse: A Study of Inquiry Reports 1980–1989*. London: HMSO.

DoH (Department of Health) (1991b) *Working Together (under the Children Act 1989)*. London: HMSO.

DoH (Department of Health) (1991c) *Working with Child Sexual Abuse: Guidelines for Trainers and Managers in Social Service Departments*. London: HMSO.

DoH (Department of Health) (1995) *Child Protection: Messages from Research*. London: HMSO.

DoH (Department of Health) (1999) *Working Together to Safeguard Children*. London: The Stationery Office.

Dominelli, L. and McLeod, E. (1989) *Feminist Social Work*. Basingstoke: Macmillan.

Dryzek, J. (1995) Critical theory as a research programme, in *The Cambridge Companion to Habermas*. Cambridge: Cambridge University Press.

Durkheim, E. (1961) *Moral Education: A Study in the Theory and Application of the Sociology of Education*. New York: Glencoe Free Press.

Elliot, M.A. and Merrill, F.E. (1961) *Social Disorganization*, 4th edn. New York: Harper.

Erikson, E. (1963) *Childhood and Society*. New York: Norton.

Etzioni, A. (1964) *Modern Organizations*. Englewood Cliffs, NJ: Prentice Hall.

Etzioni, A. (1975) *Comparative Analysis of Complex Organizations*. New York: Free Press.

Evans, M. and Miller, C. (1992) *Partnership in Child Protection: The Strategic Management Response*. London: Office for Public Management and National Institute for Social Work.

Faller, K. (1981) *Social Work with Abused and Neglected Children*. New York: Free Press.

Faller, K. (1985) Unanticipated problems in the United States child protection system, *Child Abuse and Neglect*, 9: 63–9.

Faller, K. (1988) *Child Sexual Abuse: An Interdisciplinary Manual for Diagnosis, Case Management and Treatment*. New York: Macmillan.

Family and Children's Services (1998) *Family and Children's Services 1997/98 Annual Report*, Perth: Western Australian Government.

Family Rights Group (1991) *The Children Act 1989: An FRG Briefing Pack*. London: Family Rights Group.

Featherstone, M., Hepworth, M. and Turner, B. (eds) (1993) *The Body: Social Process and Cultural Theory*. London: Sage.

Fineman, M. (1989) The politics of custody and gender: child advocacy and the transformation of custody decision making in the USA, in C. Smart and S. Sevenhuijsen (eds) *Child Custody and the Politics of Gender*, pp. 27–50. London: Routledge.

Finklehor, D. (1980) Risk factors in the sexual victimization of children, *Child Abuse and Neglect*, 4: 265–73.

Finklehor, D. (1982) Sexual abuse: a sociological perspective, *Child Abuse and Neglect*, 6: 95–102.

Finklehor, D. (ed.) (1986) *A Sourcebook on Child Sexual Abuse*. Beverly Hills, CA: Sage.

Finklehor, D. (1993) Epidemiological factors in the clinical identification of child sexual abuse, *Child Abuse and Neglect*, 17: 67–70.

Finklehor, D. and Hotaling, G.T. (1984) Sexual abuse in the national incidence study of child abuse and neglect: an appraisal, *Child Abuse and Neglect*, 8: 23–33.

Fox Harding, L.M. (1991a) The Children Act in context: four perspectives in child care law and policy (I), *Journal of Social Welfare and Family Law*, 3: 179–93.

Fox Harding, L.M. (1991b) The Children Act in context: four perspectives in child care law and policy (II), *Journal of Social Welfare and Family Law*, 4: 285–302.

Frank, A.W. (1993) For a sociology of the body: an analytic review, in M. Featherstone, M. Hepworth and S. Turner (eds) *The Body: Social Process and Cultural Theory*, pp. 36–102. London: Sage.

Franklyn, B. (ed.) (1995a) *The Handbook of Children's Rights: Comparative Policy and Practice*. London: Routledge.

Franklyn, B. (1995b) The case for children's rights: a progress report, in B. Franklyn (ed.) *The Handbook of Children's Rights: Comparative Policy and Practice*, pp. 3–21. London: Routledge.

Furniss, T. (1983) Mutual interest and interlocking professional-family process in the treatment of child sexual abuse and incest, *Child Abuse and Neglect*, 7: 207–23.

Gelles, R.J. (1987) *Family Violence*, 2nd edn. London: Sage.

Gerth, H. and Mills, C. (eds) (1947) *From Max Weber: Essays in Sociology*. New York: Oxford University Press.

Geuss, R. (1981) *The Idea of a Critical Theory: Habermas and the Frankfurt School*. Cambridge: Cambridge University Press.

Gibbins, J.R. (1998) Postmodernity, poststructuralism, in J. Carter (ed.) *Postmodernity and Fragmentation of Welfare*, pp. 31–49. London: Routledge.

Giddens, A. (1990) *The Consequences of Modernity*. Cambridge: Polity Press.

Giddens, A. (1991) *Modernity and Self-Identity: Self and Society in the Late Modern Age*. Cambridge: Polity Press.

Giddens, A. (1993) *Sociology*, 2nd edn. Oxford: Blackwell.

Giovanni, J. and Becerra, R. (1979) *Defining Child Abuse*. New York: Free Press.

Goddard, C. and Tucci, J. (1991) Child protection and the need for reappraisal of the social worker-client relationship, *Australian Social Work*, 44(2): 3–10.

Goldson, B. (1997) Childhood and introduction to historical and theoretical analysis, in P. Scarton (ed.) *Childhood in Crisis*, pp. 1–27. London: UCC Press.

Gordon, L. (1985) Child abuse, gender, and the myth of family independence: a historical critique, *Child Welfare*, LXIV(3): 213–24.

Gordon, S. (2002) *Inquiry into Response by Government Agencies to Complaints of Family Violence and Child Abuse in Aboriginal Communities*. Perth: Western Australian Government.

Gough, D. (1996) Defining the problem, *Child Abuse and Neglect*, 20(11): 993–1002.

Graburn, N. (1971) *Readings in Kinship and Social Structure*. Berkeley, CA: Harper & Row.

Griffiths, D. and Moynihan, F. (1963) Multiple epiphyseal injuries in babies, *British Medical Journal*, 5372: 1558–61.

Grimal, P. (1965) *Larousse World Mythology*. London: Paul Hamlyn.

Habermas, J. (1984) *The Theory of Communicative Action, Vol. 1: Reason and the Rationalization of Society*. Boston, MA: Beacon Press.

Habermas, J. (1987) *The Philosophical Discourse of Modernity*. Cambridge: Polity Press.

Habermas, J. (1988) *The Theory of Communicative Action, Vol. 2: Lifeworld and System – A Critique of Functionalist Reason*. Boston, MA: Beacon Press.

Hage, J. and Powers, C.H. (1992) *Post-Industrial Lives*. London: Sage.

Hall, S., Critcher, C., Jefferson, T., Clark, J. and Roberts, B. (1978) *Policing the Crisis: Mugging, the State and Law and Order*. London: Macmillan.

Hallett, C. (1993) Working together in child protection, in L. Waterhouse (ed.) *Child Abuse and Child Abusers: Protection and Prevention*, pp. 139–53. London: Jessica Kingsley.

Hallett, C. and Birchall, E. (1992) *Coordination and Child Protection: A Review of the Literature*. London: HMSO.

Hasenfeld, Y. (1983) *Human Service Organizations*. Englewood Cliffs, NJ: Prentice Hall.

Haslam, M.T. (1991) Child sexual abuse: the Cleveland experience, *Medicine and Law*, 10: 615–21.

Heffner, R.D. (trans, ed.) (1960) *Alexis de Tocqueville: Democracy in America*. New York: Mentor Books.

Hendrick, H. (1990) Constructions and reconstructions of British child-hood: an interpretive survey, 1800 to the present, in A. James and A. Prout (eds) *Constructing and Reconstructing Childhood: Contemporary Issues in the Sociological Study of Childhood*, pp. 35–59. London: Falmer Press.

Hitchcock, G. and Hughes, D. (1992) *Research and the Teacher*. London: Routledge.

HMSO (Her Majesty's Stationery Office) (1995) *County Council Yearbook*. London: HMSO.

Horwath, J. (1999) Inter-agency practice in suspected cases of Munchausen Syndrome by Proxy (Fictitious Illness by Proxy): dilemmas for professionals, *Child and Family Social Work*, 4: 109–18.

Houston, S. and Griffiths, H. (2000) Reflections on risk in child protection: is it time for a shift in paradigm? *Child and Family Social Work*, 5(1): 1–10.

Howe, D. (1992) Child abuse and the bureaucratisation of social work, *The Sociological Review*, 14(3): 491–508.

Howe, D. (1994) Modernity, postmodernity and social work, *British Journal of Social Work*, 24(5): 513–32.

Howitt, D. (1992) *Child Abuse Errors: When Good Intentions Go Wrong*. Hemel Hempstead: Wheatsheaf.

Hutchinson, E. (1993) Mandatory reporting laws: child protective case finding gone awry? *Social Work*, 38(1): 56–63.

Ife, J. (1997) *Rethinking Social Work*. Melbourne: Longman.

James, A. and Prout, A. (eds) (1990) *Constructing and Reconstructing Childhood: Contemporary Issues in the Sociological Study of Childhood*. London: Falmer Press.

Janis, I. (1975) Group think, *Psychology Today*, 5(6): 74–6.

Janis, I. (1982) *Group Think: Psychological Studies of Policy Decisions and Fiascos*. Boston, MA: Houghton Mifflin.

Jeffries, A., Hodges, V. and Chandler, J. (1995) The wishes and feelings of children. Paper presented at the conference on 'Government Policies and Their Effects on Children', University of Central Lancashire.

Jeffries, A., Hodges, V. and Chandler, J. (1997) Who's listening? The voice of children in divorce. Paper presented at the conference on 'Children and Social Competence', University of Surrey.

Jenks, C. (1996) *Childhood.* London: Routledge.

Jones, A. and Bilton, K. (1994) *The Future Shape of Children's Services.* London: The National Children's Bureau.

Jones, A. and May, J. (1995) *Working in Human Services Organisations: A Critical Approach.* Melbourne, Vic: Longman.

Jones, D. (1996) Commentary: Munchausen Syndrome by Proxy – is expansion justified? *Child Abuse and Neglect,* 20(10): 983–4.

Kadushin, A. and Martin, J. (1988) *Child Welfare Services,* 4th edn. New York: Macmillan.

Kalichman, S., Craig, M. and Follingstad, D. (1990) Professionals' adherence to mandatory child abuse reporting laws: effects of responsibility attribution, confidence ratings and situational factors, *Child Abuse and Neglect,* 14: 69–77.

Kaul, M. (1983) Physical child abuse: a controllable problem, *Paediatric Social Work,* 3(2): 39–42.

Kelly, L. (1988) From politics to pathology: the medicalization of the impact of rape and child sexual abuse, *Radical Community Medicine,* 36: 14–18.

Kelly, L. (1993) Organized sexual abuse: what do we know and what do we need to know? in Child Abuse Studies Unit, *Abuse of Women and Children: A Feminist Response.* London: University of North London Press.

Kempe, C.H. and Helfer, R.E. (eds) (1972) *Helping the Battered Child and His Family.* Philadelphia, PA: Lippencott.

Kempe, C.H., Silverman, F.N., Steele, F.B., Droegemueller, M.D. and Silver, H.K. (1962) The battered child syndrome, *Journal of the American Medical Association,* July(181): 17–24.

Kempe, R.S. (1979) Recent developments in the field of child abuse, *Child Abuse and Neglect,* 3: 9–15.

Kempe, R.S. and Kempe, C.H. (1978) *Child Abuse: The Developing Child.* London: Fontana/Open Books.

Kempe, R.S. and Kempe, C.H (1984) *The Common Secret: The Sexual Abuse of Children and Adolescents.* New York: W.H. Freeman.

King, M. (1997) *A Better World for Children.* London: Routledge.

King, M. (ed.) (1999) *Moral Agendas for Children's Welfare.* London: Routledge.

Kitzinger, J. (1990) Who are you kidding? Children, power, and the struggle against sexual abuse, in A. James and A. Prout (eds) *Constructing and Reconstructing Childhood: Contemporary Issues in the Sociological Study of Childhood,* pp. 157–83. London: Falmer Press.

Knight, C. (1991) *Blood Relations: Menstruation and the Origin of Culture.* New Haven, CT: Yale University Press.

Laming, Lord Justice H. (2003) *The Victoria Climbié Inquiry Report, CM 5730*. London: The Stationery Office.

Lansdown, G. (1995) The children's rights development unit, in B. Franklyn (ed.) *The Handbook of Children's Rights*, pp. 107–18, London: Routledge.

Lawrence, A. (1990) Child sexual assault treatment, *The West Australian Social Worker*, WBH 0847(August): 1–3.

Lawrence, A. (2001) *Interagency Coordination and Collaboration in the Management of Child Sexual Abuse*, published Ph.D. thesis, University of Plymouth.

Lawrence, A. and Harrison, C. (1994) Reporting of cases of non-accidental injury: a survey of parents' responses, *Journal of Quality Clinical Practice*, 14: 207–15.

Lawrence, D. (1996) *Self-Esteem in the Classroom*. London: Paul Chapman.

Lee, H.D. (trans) (1958) *Plato: The Republic*. London: Harmonsworth.

Leonard, P. (1997) *Postmodern Welfare*. London: Sage.

Lestor, J. (1995) A minister for children, in B. Franklyn (ed.) *Handbook of Children's Rights: Comparative Policy and Practice*, pp. 100–6. London: Routledge.

Lincoln, Y.S. and Guba, E.G. (1985) *Naturalistic Inquiry*. Beverly Hills, CA: Sage.

Lindsey, D. (1994) *The Welfare of Children*. Oxford: Oxford University Press.

Luhmann, N. (1988) The third question: the creative use of paradox in law and legal history, *Journal of Law and Society*, 15: 153.

Luhmann, N. (1990) *Essays on Self-Reference*. New York: Columbia University Press.

Lynch, M. (1986) The International Society for Prevention of Child Abuse and Neglect: the future, *Child Abuse and Neglect*, 10: 451–3.

Lyon, C. and Parton, N. (1995) Children's rights and the Children Act 1989, in B. Franklyn (ed.) *Handbook of Children's Rights: Comparative Policy and Practice*, pp. 40–55. London: Routledge.

Lyon, E. and Kouloumpos-Lenares, K. (1987) Clinician and state children's services worker collaboration, *Child Welfare*, 66(6): 517–27.

Lyotard, J.F. (1984) *The Postmodern Condition: A Report on Knowledge*. Manchester: Manchester University Press.

MacDonald, G. (1990) Allocating blame in social work, *British Journal of Social Work*, 20(6): 526–46.

McDowell, L. and Pringle, R. (1992) Defining public and private issues, in L. McDowell and R. Pringle (eds) *Defining Women: Social Institutions and Gender Divisions*, pp. 9–17. Oxford: Blackwell/Priory.

McGuinness, C. (1993) *Report of the Kilkenny Incest Investigation*. Dublin: Stationery Office.

McGuinness, C. (1996) Keynote address, 12th biennial conference of the International Society for the Prevention of Child Abuse and Neglect (ISPCAN), Dublin, Ireland.

McKenna, D. (1999) Private communication.

Marneffe, C. (1996) Child abuse treatment: a fallow land, *Child Abuse and Neglect*, 20(3): 379–84.

Martin, J. (1994) The organiszation of exclusion: institutionalization of sex inequality, gender faculty jobs and gendered knowledge in organizational theory and research, *Organization*, 1: 401–31.

May, M. (1978) Violence in the family: an historical perspective, in J.P. Martin (ed) *Violence in the Family*, pp. 135–7. Chichester: Wiley.

Mayall, B. (1996) *Children, Health and the Social Order*. Buckingham: Open University Press.

Mead, G.H. (1934) *Mind, Self and Society*. Chicago: University of Chicago Press.

Merton, R.K. (1963) *Social Theory and Social Structure*. Glencoe: Free Press.

Minuchin, S. and Fishman, H.C. (1981) *Family Therapy Techniques*. Cambridge, MA: Harvard University Press.

Molin, R. and Herskowitz, S. (1986) Clinicians and caseworkers: issues in consultation and collaboration regarding protective service clients, *Child Abuse and Neglect*, 10: 201–10.

Morris, K. and Shepherd, C. (2000) Quality social work with children and families, *Child and Family Social Work*, 5(2): 169–76.

Morrison, T. (1990) When the system is stuck: professional dangerousness and the multidisciplinary child protection management system. Paper presented at the child abuse conference, Department for Community Welfare, Perth, Western Australia.

Morrison, T. (1993) Multidisciplinary collaboration: the dreams, the dangers, the politics of practice, in The Advisory and Co-ordinating Committee on Child Abuse, *Children at Risk: The Politics of Practice*, pp. 5–29. Fremantle, Western Australia: The Advisory and Co-ordinating Committee on Child Abuse.

Morrison, T. (1996) Partnership and collaboration: rhetoric and reality, *Child Abuse and Neglect*, 20(2): 127–40.

Morrow, R. and Brown, D. (1994) *Critical Theory and Methodology*. London: Sage.

Morss, J.R. (1990) *The Biologizing of Childhood: Developmental Psychology and the Darwinian Myth*. Hove: Lawrence Erlbaum.

Mrazek, P.B. (1981) The nature of incest: a review of the contributing factors, in P.B. Mrazek and C.H. Kempe (eds) *Sexually Abused Children and their Families*, pp. 97–107. Oxford: Pergamon Press.

Mrazek, P.B. and Kempe, C.H. (eds) (1981) *Sexually Abused Children and Their Families*. Oxford: Pergamon Press.

Mrazek, P.B., Lynch, M. and Bentovim, A. (1983) Sexual abuse of children in the United Kingdom, *Child Abuse and Neglect*, 7(2): 147–53.

Mullender, A. and Perrott, S. (1998) Social work and organisations, in R. Adams, L. Dominelli and M. Payne (eds) *Social Work: Themes, Issues and Critical Debates*, pp. 67–77. London: Macmillan Press.

Myers, J.E.B. (ed.) (1994) *The Backlash: Child Protection Under Fire*. London: Sage.

Newell, P. (1995) Respecting children's rights to physical integrity, in B. Franklyn (ed.) *Handbook of Children's Rights*, pp. 215–26. London: Routledge.

O'Hagan, K. (1989) *Working With Child Sexual Abuse*. Buckingham: Open University Press.

O'Hagan, K. and Dillenburger, K. (1995) *The Abuse of Women Within Childcare Work*. Buckingham: Open University Press.

Parton, C. and Parton, N. (1989) Child protection: the law and dangerousness, in O. Stevenson (ed.) *Child Abuse: Public Policy and Professional Practice*, pp. 54–73. Hemel Hempstead: Harvester Wheatsheaf.

Parton, N. (1985) *The Politics of Child Abuse*. London: Macmillan.

Parton, N. (1991) *Governing the Family*. London: Macmillan.

Parton, N. (1994) Problematics of government: (post)modernity and social work, *British Journal of Social Work*, 24(1): 9–32.

Parton, N. (1997) *Child Protection and Family Support: Tensions, Contradictions and Possibilities*. London: Routledge.

Parton, N. (1998) Risk, advanced liberalism and child welfare: the need to rediscover uncertainty and ambiguity, *British Journal of Social Work*, 28: 5–27.

Parton, N. and Marshall, W. (1998) Postmodernism and discourse approaches to social work, in R. Adams, L. Dominelli and M. Payne (eds) *Social Work: Themes, Issues and Critical Debates*, pp. 240–9. London: Macmillan.

Parton, N., Thorpe, D. and Wattam, C. (1997) *Child Protection: Risk and Moral Order*. London: Macmillan.

Payne, M. (1982) *Working in Teams*. London: Macmillan.

Payne, M. (1998) Social work theories and reflective practice, in R. Adams, L. Dominelli and M. Payne (eds) *Social Work: Themes, Issues and Critical Debates*, pp. 117–37. London: Macmillan.

Perrow, C. (1979) *Complex Organizations*. Glenview, IL: Scott, Foresman.

Perrow, C. (1986) *Complex Organization: A Critical Essay*, 3rd edn. New York: Random House.

Piaget, J. (1974) *Understanding Causality*. New York: Norton.

Pidgeon, N. (1997) Grounded theory: theoretical background, in J.T.E. Richardson (ed.) *Handbook of Qualitative Research Methods*, pp. 75–85. Leicester: The British Psychological Society.

Piper, C. (1999) Moral campaigns for children's welfare in the nineteenth century, in M. King (ed.) *Moral Agendas for Children's Welfare*, pp. 33–52. New York: Routledge.

Pizzini, S. (1994) The backlash from the perspective of a county child protective services administrator, in J. Meyers (ed.) *The Backlash: Child Protection Under Fire*, pp. 31–46. London: Sage.

Potter, J. (1997) Discourse analysis and constructionist approaches: theoretical background, in J.T.E. Richardson (ed.) *Handbook of Qualitative Research Methods*, pp. 125–40. Leicester: The British Psychological Society.

Powell, M. (1991) Investigating and reporting child sexual abuse: review and recommendations for clinical practice, *Australian Psychologist*, 26(2): 77–83.

Pusey, M. (1995) *Jurgen Habermas*. London: Routledge.

Ray, L. (1993) *Rethinking Critical Theory: Emancipation in the Age of Social Movements*. London: Sage.

Rayner, M. (1995) Children's rights in Australia, in B. Franklyn (ed.) *Handbook of Children's Rights: Comparative Policy and Practice*, pp. 188–200. London: Routledge.

Reder, P., Duncan, S. and Gray, M. (1993) *Beyond Blame: Child Abuse Tragedies Revisited*. London: Routledge.

Reid, C. (1989) *Mothers of Sexually Abused Girls: A Feminist View (Social Work Monographs)*. Norwich: University of East Anglia.

Richardson, J.T.E. (ed.) (1997) *Handbook of Qualitative Research Methods*. Leicester: The British Psychological Society.

Risin, L.I. and McNamara, J.R. (1989) Validation of child sexual abuse: the psychologist's role, *Journal of Clinical Psychology*, 45(1): 175–84.

Robin, M. (ed.) (1991) *Assessing Child Maltreatment Reports: The Problem of False Allegations*. New York: Haworth Press.

Robins, S. (1990) *Organisation Theory: Design and Applications*, 3rd edn. Englewood Cliffs, NJ: Prentice Hall.

Rogers, C. (1951) *Client Centered Therapy*. London: Constable.

Rowbotham, S. (1989) Impediments to equality, in *The Past is Before Us: Feminism in Action since the 1960s*, pp. 165–81. Harmondsworth: Penguin.

Russell, D. (1983) The incidence and prevalence of intrafamilial and extrafamilial sexual abuse of female children, *Child Abuse and Neglect*, 7: 133–46.

Sanders, R., Jackson, S. and Thomas, N. (1996) The balance of prevention investigation and treatment in the management of child protection services, *Child Abuse and Neglect*, 20(10): 899–906.

Sarup, M. (1993) *An Introductory Guide to Post-structuralism and Postmodernism*, 2nd edn. Hemel Hempstead: Harvester Wheatsheaf.

Sarup, M. (1996) *Identity, Culture and the Postmodern World*. Edinburgh: Edinbrugh University Press.

Satir, V. (1967) *Conjoint Family Therapy*, revised edn. Palo Alto, CA: Science and Behaviour Books.

Schechter, M.D. and Roberge, L. (1976) Sexual exploitation, in R.E. Helfer and C.H. Kempe (eds) *Child Abuse and Neglect: The Family and the Community*, pp. 127–42. Cambridge, MA: Ballinger.

Schreier, H.A. (1996) Repeated false allegations of sexual abuse presenting to sheriffs: when is it Munchausen By Proxy? *Child Abuse and Neglect*, 20(10): 985–91.

Scott, D. (1997) Interagency conflict: an ethnographic study, *Child and Family Social Work*, 2(2): 73–80.

Sgroi, S.M. (ed.) (1982) *Handbook of Clinical Intervention in Child Sexual Abuse*. Lexington, MA: Lexington Books.

Shilling, C. (1993) *The Body and Social Theory*. London: Sage.

Silverman, D. (1970) *The Theory of Organizations*. London: Heinemann.

Skaff, L.F. (1988) Child maltreatment coordinating committees for effective service delivery, *Child Welfare*, LXVII(3): 217–31.

Skehill, C., O'Sullivan, E. and Buckley, H. (1999) The nature of child protection practices: an Irish casestudy, *Child and Family Social Work*, 4(2): 145–52.

Skinner, B.F. (1953) *Science and Human Behaviour*. New York: Macmillan.

Smart, C. (1989) Power and the politics of child custody, in C. Smart and S. Sevenhuijsen (eds) *Child Custody and the Politics of Gender*, pp. 1–27. London: Routledge.

Smart, C. (1990) *Feminism and the Power of the Law*. London: Routledge.

Smart, C. and Sevenhuijsen, S. (eds) (1989) *Child Custody and the Politics of Gender*. London: Routledge.

Smith, C. and White, S. (1997) Parton, Howe and postmodernity: a critical comment on mistaken identity, *British Journal of Social Work*, 27: 275–95.

Spratt, T., Houston, S. and Magill, T. (2000) Imaging the future: theatre and change within the child protection system, *Child and Family Social Work*, 5(2): 117–217.

Stanley, J. and Goddard, C. (1993) The effect of child abuse and other family violence on the child protection worker and case management, *Australian Social Work*, 46(3): 3–10.

Starr, R.H. (ed.) (1982) *Child Abuse Prediction: Policy Implications*. Cambridge, MA: Ballinger.

Stevenson, O. (1989a) The challenge of interagency collaboration, *Adoption and Fostering*, 13(1): 31–8.

Stevenson, O. (ed.) (1989b) *Child Abuse: Public Policy and Professional Practice*. Hemel Hempstead: Harvester Wheatsheaf.

Summitt, R.C. (1988) Hidden victims, hidden pain: societal avoidance of child sexual abuse, in G.E. Wyatt and G.J. Powell (eds) *Lasting Effects of Child Sexual Abuse*. Newbury Park, CA: Sage.

Taylor-Gooby, P. (1994) Postmodernism and social policy: a great leap backwards, *Journal of Social Policy*, 23(3): 385–405.

Theunissen, C.A.G. and Lusnats, G.H.A. (1994) On the development of a specialist child sexual abuse treatment programme in marriage guidance Western Australia Inc: the establishment of the inappropriate sexual contact in families programme, in Advisory and Co-ordinating Committee on Child Abuse, *Children at Risk: the Politics of Practice*, pp. 181–99. Fremantle, Western Australia: Advisory and Co-ordinating Committee on Child Abuse.

Thorpe, D. (1994) *Evaluating Child Protection*. Buckingham: Open University Press.

Thorpe, D. and Jackson, M. (1997) Child protection services and parental reactions to children's behaviour, *Child and Family Social Work*, 2(2): 81–9.

Toren, C. (1997) Ethnography: theoretical background, in J.T.E. Richardson (ed.) *Handbook of Qualitative Research Methods*, pp. 102–12. Leicester: The British Psychological Society.

Turner, B.S. (1992) Periodization and politics in the postmodern, in B.S. Turner (ed.) *Theories of Modernity and Postmodernity*, pp. 1–13. London: Sage.

Turner, B.S. (1994) *Regulating Bodies*. London: Routledge.

United Nations (1959) *Declaration of the Rights of the Child*, Resolution 1386 (XIV) of 20. Geneva: United Nations.

United Nations (1989) *Declaration of the Rights of the Child*, Resolution 1386 (XIV), in *Yearbook of the United Nations*. New York: United Nations.

Van Vucht Tijssen, L. (1992) Women between modernity and postmodernity, in B.S. Turner (ed.) *Theories of Modernity and Postmodernity*, pp. 147–63.

Vittachi, A. (1989) *Stolen Childhood: In Search of the Rights of Children*. Oxford: Blackwell/Polity Press.

Vizard, E., Monck, E. and Misch, P. (1995) Child and adolescent sex abuse perpetrators: a review of the research literature, *Journal of Child Psychology and Psychiatry*, 36(5): 731–56.

Watson, C. (1989) *Playing the State: Australian Feminist Interventions*. London: Verso.

Watson, J.B. (1924) *Psychology from the Standpoint of a Behaviourist*. Philadelphia, PA: Lippencott.

Wattam, C. (1992) *Making a Case in Child Protection*. London: Longman.

Wattam, C. (1996) The social construction of child abuse for practical purposes – a review of *Child Protection: Messages from Research*, *Child and Family Law Quarterly*, 18(3): 189–200.

Weber, M. (1946) *From Max Weber: Essays in Sociology*. London: Routledge & Kegan Paul.

Westcott. H. (1995) Perceptions of child protection casework: views from children, parents and practitioners, in C. Cloke and M. Davies (eds) *Participation and Empowerment in Child Protection*. London: Pitman Publishing.

Wolfe, D.E. and Wolfe, D.A. (1988) The sexually abused child, in E.S. Mash and L.G. Terdall (eds) *Behavioural Assessment of Childhood Disorders*, 2nd edn. New York: Guildford Press.

Wyvill, L.F. (1991) *Royal Commission into Aboriginal Black Deaths in Custody*. Canberra: Australian Government.

Yapko, M. (1997) The troublesome unknowns about traumas and recovered memories, in M. Conway (ed.) *Recovered Memories and False Memories*, pp. 23–33. Oxford: Oxford University Press.

Zeedyk, M.S. (1998) Parent-infant interaction: interpreting meaning in infants' actions, in C.A. Niven and A. Walker (eds) *Current Issues in Infancy and Parenthood*, pp. 158–78. London: Butterworth Heinemann.

Index